THE TOWNHOUSE MASSACRE

THE UNFORGETTABLE CRIMES OF RICHARD SPECK

RYAN GREEN

For Helen, Harvey, Frankie and Dougie

Disclaimer

This book is about real people committing real crimes. The story has been constructed by facts but some of the scenes, dialogue and characters have been fictionalised.

Polite Note to the Reader

This book is written in British English except where fidelity to other languages or accents are appropriate. Some words and phrases may differ from US English.

YOUR FREE BOOK IS WAITING

From bestselling author Ryan Green

There is a man who is officially classed as **"Britain's most dangerous prisoner"**

The man's name is Robert Maudsley, and his crimes earned him the nickname **"Hannibal the Cannibal"**

This free book is an exploration of his story...

★★★★★ *"Ryan brings the horrifying details to life. I can't wait to read more by this author!"*

Get a free copy of ***Robert Maudsley: Hannibal the Cannibal*** when you sign up to join my Reader's Group.

www.ryangreenbooks.com/free-book

CONTENTS

The Tyranny of Whores

Shirley Anne Speck was a whore, and that was all there was to it. No, not Speck. Malone. That bitch didn't deserve to carry the same name as Richard's saint of a mother. How dare she treat him this way? Leaving him just because he wasn't around for a few days. It wasn't like he wanted to be away when the baby squirted out of her — he was locked up. How was it fair to punish him for something the cops had done? It wasn't. It was just an excuse. Whores would take any excuse to get out of their marital duties, flaunting it around town, trying to get somebody better. There was nobody better than Richard. Nobody. When would these whores learn?

Some treacherous little voice penetrated the alcoholic haze to remind him that he wasn't strictly telling the truth there. Mary Margaret Speck wasn't nearly as saintly as he'd have liked her to be. He wasn't a virgin birth. His seven siblings weren't either. Then there was that peg-legged bastard that came around after Dad dropped dead. He must have been giving it to her good to make her forget all the abuse he heaped on her and the kids. She must have been moaning and flopping underneath him every night for her to turn a blind eye to the way little Richard cringed every time old peg-leg opened his mouth to spit out his poison.

Richard cringed away from that image of his mother spread out on a bed like a whore. But why? Why was he hiding from the truth? This was what all women were like. This was all that they wanted. To hurt him, betray him and toss his memory away the moment they had the opportunity. It had happened to Dad, and it was happening to him, too. He'd barely been gone a week, and already Shirley had moved on. She'd taken his kid from him. She'd taken the roof from over his head. He'd come out of prison expecting a welcome party, and all he got was the cold shoulder from everybody. What was he supposed to do? Just take it lying down when some prick in a bar took a swing at him? Would he have been the man Shirley married if he'd done a thing like that? No. She'd have never let him live it down. He wouldn't have been able to stand the sight of himself. She would've wanted him to hit the guy. Maybe pull his knife. That was what she wanted. So why was she acting like she didn't?

Whores, every last one of them. Just waiting for a chance to slither into some other man's bed. It didn't matter if the other man was better or worse — they just wanted somebody. It wasn't right, the way that women treated men. It wasn't right that these whores got to lord it over everyone, deciding who gets what and when. Why did a whore have more rights than him? Why did that whore Shirley get to decide that he wasn't allowed to live in his own apartment anymore? That he didn't get to lie down in bed with her the way that she was meant to lie down as her husband demanded. The world was all wrong, and these whores were to blame, turning men's heads and making them do whatever they were asked in exchange for a taste. It shouldn't be this way. Somebody ought to put things right. Put those whores back in their place. Let them know that they were beneath men and that they were meant to get beneath men whenever they were told.

Richard had a knife. He'd always carried one for as long as he could remember. Sometimes a fight went south, and you wanted something to turn it around. Sometimes you needed to part a man from his money with the minimum amount of trouble. That was what being a man was all about — strength. He was strong, and other men were weak, so he could take what he wanted from them. That was the natural order of things, and if women would just obey that natural order, then everything would've been fine. But they didn't. Women were slick and slippery. They could slide around the side of what you were saying and twist your own words around to make you look stupid. They could lift up their skirts and make any man go weak. It didn't matter to them that Richard was stronger than them because they had that secret power over men that let them ruin everything whenever it took their fancy. He was done bowing down to it. He was tired of the tyranny of whores. He wasn't going to go sniffing around their skirts and begging them for what he wanted anymore. He was strong. They were weak. And the rules applied to them just the same as everyone else. Whores would give him what he wanted, or he'd cut up their pretty faces. He'd squeeze their soft necks until they all went blue. He was in control now. He was the one with the power.

His hand rested on the knife in his belt as he finished up the last dregs of rotgut whiskey in his glass. He could feel the texture of the wooden handle, the grain, the reassuring weight of it. He didn't need the approval of whores when he had this. He was strong. He'd never felt stronger. When he rose up from the barstool, he nearly toppled, but a few steps towards the door put him into a rhythm, and that gave him his balance. He'd been drinking for as long as he could piss standing up; he knew how to handle his liquor. When he stepped out into the cool night, it washed the worst of his drunkenness away. The swaying stopped, his stumbling steps became steady. Stepping out into the darkness was like waking up. The warm feelings of the bar hadn't left him, but he was wearing them, instead of the other way around, wrapping that cotton-wool around himself as insulation from the cruel world out there.

Weak men would have been weeping about now, but Richard had learned to channel all his misery into anger.

Sobbing never helped anything. Getting angry did. Angry men got things done. He had an enemy, and he hit them. He had a barrier; he smashed through it. It was what he'd always done, and what he'd always do when a problem presented itself. But tonight's problem — the problem of whores — was altogether too abstract to present such a simple solution. He couldn't break all the whores of their bad habits in one night. He couldn't round them all up and re-educate them in the correct way to treat a man. It just wasn't practical. He needed something that he could do right now, something to set the world back on its right course, to knock the whores from their reeking thrones and put men back where they belonged, at the top of the food chain. He had to do something. Set some example. He needed to let the whores know that one man in the entire world wasn't scared of them. He wasn't afraid they might snatch away their filthy offerings. They'd already taken everything from him, and he was still standing. They had nothing left in their handbags of tricks.

As his mind wandered through the spiky maze of his drunken fury, his legs carried him on unguided into the city night. There were few people out this late and this far from the safe neon lights of the main streets, but here and there, he caught a glimpse of them in the lamplight. The homeless, the police, more drunks staggering home just like he should've been, if he'd had a home to stagger back to. Men, just trying to live their lives under the oppressive thumb of the whores. He sank back into his reverie and drifted a few more blocks, circling slowly back towards the bar.

She'd been gone when he got out of prison the first time around after that bar fight put him away. That had been a bad time in his life — no welcome party, no smiles, no wife, no kid. The whore had upped sticks and left him before he'd even met the brat. He could forgive her leaving during the next sentence — a year and a half was a long time to wait — but those few weeks back then? That was unconscionable. How cruel did a whore have to be to treat a loving and kind man like that? A man who'd done nothing to her but put food on the table and a roof over her head, when he remembered to go to work.

Running away after he got locked up that first time was wicked. He'd never forgive it, but it wasn't nearly as bad as what came after. When he went crawling home from jail to his momma and his sister, both those filthy whores had taken the other whore's side. They wouldn't tell him where she'd gone. They wouldn't help him reclaim what was rightfully his. They were the worst ones, those two whores. Those two betrayers. He'd never speak to them again if he could help it. Whores siding with whores against the men they ought to love above all others. It was despicable.

This latest betrayal, the news that she'd shacked up with somebody else even though the government still said they were married, that was what had brought all the old bitterness back. He was so willing to forgive and forget, but the whore just kept on twisting the knife that she'd jammed in his back. She just wouldn't let him rest for even a moment. She was intent on keeping him suffering. It wasn't right. It wasn't fair. He hadn't done a thing to deserve it.

When he blinked his blurred vision away — not tears, just a little bleariness from the booze — Richard realised he'd made some wrong turns along the way. The bar was nowhere near here. He had wandered close to suburbia. There were condos all around. It was quiet out here, too quiet by far for his tastes. It made the hair on the back of his neck stand up, like he was just waiting for something to happen, some sound to fill up the silence. He was turning to leave and seek out someplace less unsettling when he saw her walking to her car. A whore. Strolling around at two in the morning, she had to be a whore. No good woman would be out at a time like this, no mother or virgin would risk themselves in the dark of the night. This was a whore, just like all the other whores who'd wronged him, and this was his opportunity to make an example of her.

In a few brisk steps, he closed the distance from the edge of the car park to her spot. In that same flurry of motion, he drew the knife from his belt. She must have caught a reflected shimmer of the steel in her car window because he could've sworn he didn't make a sound. She didn't look like the other whores he'd known, with her pretty blonde hair and her eyes bulging wide, but she was one. He knew in his gut that she was. He lifted the knife and got ready to make his statement, to show them all that he wasn't going to take it anymore. Then she screamed.

All the silence was stripped away. All the warmth and power that the whiskey had tricked him with vanished in a rush of cold adrenaline. The scream carried out and echoed off the walls of the condos. Lights started to go on in the windows. They were going to see him. They were going to stare at him, just like this whore was staring now. With a gasp, he turned and ran as fast as his legs could carry him. He ran and ran until the air in his lungs felt like fire, and still he tried to go faster. He was two blocks away when he ran straight into the side of a police cruiser.

It just wasn't his night.

Catalysts

On 6 December 1941, mere hours before the Japanese attack on Pearl Harbor dragged the USA into the Second World War, a smaller horror was born. Richard Benjamin Speck was the seventh of eight children, born in the tiny village of Kirkwood, Illinois. Shortly after the baby was born, the family relocated to Monmouth, Illinois, a town that Richard would consider 'home' for most of his life. His father, Benjamin, had found work in Monmouth as a warehouse packer at the Western Stoneware company, the latest in a long line of hard manual labour jobs that the 47-year-old had held throughout his life, ranging from farming to logging.

A long time had passed since the Speck family had last been blessed with a child. All of Richard's brothers and sisters were much older than him, and he lived his first few years in relative isolation from the rest of his family, with only his doting mother for company, until two years later when his sister Carolyn arrived. The two of them were company for one another through those early years in their crowded but disciplined house.

Religion hung over them all like a leaden weight. Each time any one of them even considered acting out, the threat of a more eternal punishment seemed to weigh down on them. The spokesperson for God in the household was Richard's mother, Mary Margaret Speck. She was a devout woman, teetotal and devoted to religion as much as to her family. Benjamin didn't speak of his religious beliefs so often or so openly, but he was also a man of profound faith. It was his example that Richard sought to follow, even in those early days. He found his mother's attention cloying and overwhelming compared to the quiet dignity of his father, and in his youngest son, Benjamin finally seemed to discover a kindred spirit, too. There was a closeness between the pair, in their unspoken bond full of comfortable silences that the rest of the family just didn't understand. Mary, in particular, was perturbed at the shine her husband had taken to the boy when he'd more or less allowed all his other children to be raised by her exclusively.

The nest was rapidly emptying. Their eldest daughter, Sara, was married off, and their eldest son, Robert, had moved out to start a life of his own. Mary became ever more protective of her youngest children, trying to keep them as babies for as long as possible, and sobbing when it was time for them to start school.

It was at school that young Richard encountered the first real adversity in his life. He struggled to read and seemed inattentive to the lessons, while otherwise being a quiet and polite boy. It was only with some experimentation with seating arrangements that the teacher realised that the boy was in dire need of glasses to see the blackboard. His parents were contacted, and glasses were acquired, but he refused to wear them unless his father specifically ordered him to put them on, which he rarely did, as he saw the discomfort they were causing the boy. Richard still tried to follow his father's stoic example in all things, and he felt certain that his father would never wear glasses or admit to any weakness of his makeup.

Worst still for Richard, when he wore his glasses, he drew attention from the other children in his class. He couldn't tolerate attention. He was deathly embarrassed at being the focus of others, to the point that he couldn't stand up and read in class as he was required because of the shame that it brought him. Whether this came from the isolation of his early life or some desire to emulate his taciturn father isn't clear, but the focus of his shame soon shifted to the lady schoolteacher who was forcing him into speaking. All of his misery at the attention was blamed on her.

It seems likely that he could've worked through this mental block with the help of his beloved mentor, Benjamin, but one day, he returned from school to find his father missing. In itself, this wasn't too irregular — his father took overtime shifts wherever he could get them, to put some extra cash into the family coffers — but today, his mother was missing, too. He had always somewhat resented her hovering presence in the house, always fussing over him, but now that she was absent, he felt dread settling in his stomach. Something was wrong. She was always here, and now she wasn't. Richard was six years old, and the house was empty.

His fear was not abated when Sara and her husband abruptly showed up in their car — if anything, it was made even worse. His mother might have run out to the store. He might have conjured up any number of plausible reasons that everything might still be all right if Sara hadn't shown up and wrapped him in a hug, which he couldn't even feel through his numbness.

He had made it all the way to the hospital before anyone thought to tell the boy what was happening. Benjamin Speck was dead. He'd had a heart attack in the warehouse, been rushed to the hospital and passed away as they frantically tried to get his heart beating steady again. The children had lost their father, Mary had lost her husband and Richard had lost his whole world.

He spent the next three years completely desolate, clinging to every memory of the man he'd loved, and ingraining ever deeper his discomfort with the women that controlled every aspect of his life. His mother, sisters and schoolteachers had moved on with their lives as though nothing had happened.

They'd buried Benjamin and kept on living, but Richard didn't know how to do that.

The troubles that he had at school continued to worsen, with him slipping ever further behind his classmates as he refused to read aloud in class or wear his glasses. His enmity towards his teachers moved beyond sullen disobedience to more open obstinance. Even the work that he was able to do he sometimes refused out of spite. His reputation as a good boy with troubles began to fade, and he was considered more and more often to be a problem child. Still, there was no catalyst for any further transformation, and it was quite possible that he could've righted himself given enough time and with a little socialisation outside of the family home.

Sadly, this was not to be. The second blow fell in the third year after Benjamin's death when Richard was nine years old. While travelling back home from a trip to Chicago, his mother met a man on the train. Carl Lindberg was everything that Benjamin hadn't been. He was a fast-talking travelling salesman who could charm any woman that he met, and he laid that charm on thick with Mary. In another contrast to Benjamin, Carl was a big fan of alcohol, guzzling it down and smoking like a chimney throughout the entire journey. Despite this obvious clash with her own teetotal morals, Mary was so taken with the man that she invited him home to meet her family, where he launched into a whole new sales spiel for himself, no longer just pitching himself as a lover for Mary but also as a replacement father for the kids. The older children bought it hook, line and sinker. Even Carolyn, usually shy with strangers, took to Carl almost immediately. The only one who kept his distance was Richard. He tried to stare the man down but ended up doing little more than squinting, and when Carl realised that he wasn't going to win the boy over, he just stopped trying, dismissing Richard from his thoughts entirely and putting the energy he might have wasted into charming the rest of the family. Mary was smitten, and if Richard didn't approve, well, that was likely just the loyalty to his father shining through all over again.

They conducted most of their courtship behind closed doors and far away, out of sight of the kids, and Richard found his care being passed more and more often to his eldest sister. Sara actually seemed to care deeply for her younger siblings and did her level best to keep them content while her mother went out courting, but now more than ever, Richard saw her as a jailor as often as a saviour. His mother and sister were the only adults left in his life that he cared about, and they seemed to be conspiring together to replace his father.

In early May of 1950, the whole family took a train ride down to Palo Pinto, Texas, in their church clothes. Once again, a huge event was happening in Richard's life without him having any warning or knowledge of it until it was too late. They went straight from the train station to the church where their mother was waiting, and Richard had to sit in silent horror as his mother gave herself, body and soul, to some scumbag Texan salesman that she'd met just a few weeks before. Even when the minister stopped in his rambling and asked if there was anyone present who could give a good reason that the two of them should not be wed and Richard felt the bile bubbling up in his throat, he still couldn't bring himself to stand up and speak with so many people watching. He wanted to scream. He wanted to point to his mother and curse her for this betrayal. Instead, he sat in simmering silence and wiped his tears of frustration away with his shirt cuff.

Adding insult to injury, as a part of the paperwork that they signed that day, Carl adopted all of Mary's children as a part of the ceremony. On paper, he'd become Richard's father, completely replacing Benjamin in every way that mattered. All of the rest, Richard might've been able to forgive, but not that. Every time he was called Richard Lindberg, he loathed it. Every time he even looked at Carl, rage bubbled up within him. For all that his mother wasn't particularly bothered about her son's opinion on the matter, she still wanted to keep the peace in her new household for as long as possible. So when the wedding was over, Richard and Carolyn were loaded right back onto the train alongside Sara and sent back to Monmouth.

Ostensibly, they were returning to the town so that they could finish out the school year before transferring to Texas for the next term, but everyone hoped that some time away from Carl might give Richard long enough to gain a little perspective on his whole situation. It didn't. When he saw the sign in his yard announcing that their house had been sold, he sunk into the darkest depression that his family had ever seen, not even talking to Carolyn, who could usually coax him out of any foul mood. His father was dead, and every part of his memory was being stripped away a piece at a time. First, his body had been buried. Then his name had been stripped away from the family. Now the home where they'd lived together, and made so many memories, was gone without a word. All that Richard had left of his father was a rapidly fading memory — he couldn't even picture the man's face anymore.

If he'd been failing in class before, then what he did during that brief term could barely even be called attending. He would go to the school because Sara asked him to, but that was the extent of his participation. He didn't work; he didn't socialise. He barely even acknowledged when any of the teachers spoke to him. He was on a trajectory for complete 'failure of the year', but everyone knew that he was moving state, and nobody wanted to be the cause for any more confusion and grief in that family, so he was allowed to move on without much more than a black mark on his records.

The journey to Texas was filled with trepidation for young Richard. He had no idea what to expect when he arrived — whether his new father would hold a grudge for the way that Richard had snubbed him, whether his new life, so far from everything that he knew, would ever be as good as the fading memories that he clung to.

As he stared out of the window of the train, holding Carolyn's hand, even the land he walked on seemed to be transforming, all of the rich green of Illinois fading to browns and yellows as the sun beat down on them relentlessly. He was moving from a bustling town with people everywhere to Santo, Texas, a rural village almost sixty miles out from Fort Worth. Even the air tasted different as he disembarked the train, but nothing would transform as much as Carl Lindberg was about to.

In the comfort of his own home, Carl let all of the pretences that he wore for the outside world drop away. He rolled up his trouser legs to expose the peg that replaced one of his shins and eased his prosthetic off whenever it got too warm and sweaty, which was often. His casual drinking and smoking also became considerably more serious when he was behind closed doors. The house in Santo was littered with so many empty whiskey bottles that even the organisationally obsessed Mary couldn't keep up with them all. Every room had an ashtray, stuffed to overflowing, and it filled the whole house with the stench of stale tobacco. Carl infected the whole house with his presence. While Carl made considerably more money than Benjamin in his sales job, the family was worse off than ever before. What he didn't drink or smoke, he squandered, and Mary, ever the diligent wife, didn't even think to complain about his behaviour.

Now that the deal was sealed, Carl felt safe to let his façade slip, and between some of his drunken stories and the hushed whispers of the other townsfolk, a very different picture of the dashing salesman was painted. Carl had a criminal record that encompassed forgery and drunk driving, although neither should have been surprising as he was an inveterate liar and an obvious alcoholic. None of this was a shock to Richard, who had pegged the man as a charlatan the first time that he laid eyes on him, but each new piece of news about her new beau devastated Mary anew. She'd thought she was creating a new, better life for her family, when in fact, she'd just shackled herself to a man who manipulated her emotions the way she would knead dough.

For all of that, Carl wasn't a cruel man, at least not towards Mary, whom he did seem to love in his way, nor to Carolyn, whom he doted on, bringing her home cheap little trinkets and knick-knacks from his travels. He reserved all of his vitriol for the one member of the Speck family who'd held out against him. He was a petty and spiteful man at his core, and this boy that'd been brought under his roof was so riddled with flaws that it was hard not to pick at them, just a little. It would start with a comment here or there, genuine advice on how the boy might improve himself. Then, when that was met with resentful silence, it would escalate to cutting comments and insults. Never anything too harsh, never anything that his mother might finally pipe up and object to, but a steady barrage of cruelty that undercut whatever little self-confidence the young Richard had ever managed to develop.

All of the anger that Richard had been harbouring up until this point in his life, all the impotent rage, finally had a face — the sneering drunk who couldn't have been further from the quiet dignity of his real father.

That first year with Carl in Santo was the most miserable of Richard's entire life, with all of the self-loathing that he'd experienced to date finally finding a voice — a voice that would dog his footsteps, whispering in his ear for the rest of his life because, ultimately, all of the horrible little jibes that Carl was making towards him were based on truth, and that made them all the more painful. He was a strange-looking, gawky child. He struggled to speak when he was spoken to. He was embarrassed easily, particularly around women, for reasons that he couldn't yet explain. All of the little flaws in his personality, Carl picked at and pried open until the boy skulked out in sullen silence, trying to keep the tears pricking his eyes from being seen.

Every day, Carl sniped at Richard, but it was only when he made some snide remark about the boy's dead father that Richard finally sprang into action, swinging his fists at the man feebly. Carl laughed it off, pushing the boy to the kitchen floor easily and mocking the child for his weakness. It drove him over the edge. Richard snatched a hammer from his stepfather's rarely used toolbox and swung for his skull. Carl slapped the hammer away with a laugh, but the consequences were anything but funny. His casual backhand rebounded the hammer into the 10-year-old's skull.

Richard flopped unconscious to the ground, and in an instant, Carl was up and moving. There was no way that anybody would believe this was an accident. He'd never hidden his contempt for the boy, even in public, and even if he had, Richard's loathing of him was abundantly obvious at a glance. Everyone would blame him. He'd lose Mary. He'd lose everything. All for some brat he'd never even wanted. He dropped down onto his knee and stump over the boy and slapped him across the face. 'Wake up!'

The boy didn't stir. His eyes were rolled up into his head. There was spittle frothing up out of his mouth. The flush of rage had been replaced with an eerie, deathlike pallor. But, he was still breathing. The blow hadn't killed him, and that meant Carl wasn't a murderer yet.

He slapped the kid a few more times then rolled him onto his side when he started to retch. That was probably a good sign — dying kids couldn't throw up. Carl didn't have a clue what to do. His lost leg had allowed him to dodge the draft during the Second World War, so he'd never been anywhere near a dead body. He was in uncharted territory here. So, he stayed there, kneeling over the little boy he hated until the kid started to breathe like normal again, and eventually, his dull eyes opened. Carl huffed out a sigh of relief. 'Don't ever try that shit again, or you'll get it a lot worse, you hear me?'

Richard's face contorted into a rictus of pure hatred, but he was up and moving again, scrabbling away through the puddle of his own vomit to run out of the house, away from the loathsome man who'd just dealt him the traumatic brain injury that would haunt him throughout the rest of his life.

Born to Raise Hell

The only constant in the next few years of Richard's life was change. After their single year of settling into their new living situation in Santo, Carl had them on the move again, following his usual pattern of jumping from one low-rent apartment to the next without pause or consideration.

In 1951, they settled in East Dallas, bouncing around temporary accommodation in a variety of atrocious neighbourhoods. Mary took it all stoically, but the children were constantly dismayed at the new depths of depravity that their new stepfather was dragging them into. Even after their confrontation in the Santo house, Carl still couldn't bring himself to stop abusing Richard at every opportunity, but for the first time, he'd recognised the dangers that might be involved in antagonising the child past his limits. He travelled more often for his work, did his drinking in bars instead of at the kitchen table, and became more distant from his new wife.

Neither Richard nor Carl ever spoke of the incident with the hammer, and when his mother had asked him about the horrific bruise that had spread down his face, Richard claimed to have fallen from a tyre swing onto a tree root down by the pond. But, even when the pain and the discolouration had faded, the impact of that blow did not. Richard's temper, which had always been carefully restrained in memory of his stoic father, now ran wild. He still couldn't stand attention, but now he would lash out at anyone who he felt was staring at him, in a way that he would've once considered unconscionable.

This new, emotional, Richard came to the fore in early 1952, when news arrived from back in Illinois about his oldest brother, Robert. He had been riding his motorcycle to work as usual when a drunk driver hit him. He was dead on arrival at the hospital. It brought all of Richard's old misery about his father's death back to haunt him again. He hadn't seen his older brother since they'd moved to Texas, and in some strange way, he felt like their absence had caused his death, as though his being back in Illinois could've prevented this turn of events from coming to pass. For this, as with every other hardship, he blamed Carl.

But as much as Richard despised his stepfather, the man still maintained an undue influence over the way that the boy thought. He was the only example of male adulthood that Richard had access to in his world populated by domineering women, and it was Carl's terrible example that he began to follow from the age of 12 onwards.

There was always alcohol around the house — leftover dregs in whiskey bottles; forgotten beers tucked away in the icebox, even whole bottles of liquor that Carl had forgotten that he'd bought to start with. Richard tried them all, and when that ran dry, he had the good fortune to be situated in the middle of all of the worst neighbourhoods in Dallas every time that he looked up. There was booze available everywhere, and stronger medicine, too — pills and powders to take the sting of his misery away, to fill him up with a sense of pride and power. His addiction to a whole variety of narcotics started in childhood, and it only got worse as he grew older, both because he had more money readily available and because more dealers were willing to talk to him once he looked like he might be an adult.

His school attendance began to falter as he spent more and more of his time drunk or drugged out of his mind. In 1955, at the age of 13, he was arrested for the first time. When he'd too much to drink, or had taken some new pill that was sending him on a magical journey that he wanted to experience alone, Richard would frequently break into the partially constructed housing projects that littered East Dallas and use them for shelter. His 1955 arrest was for trespassing during one of his 'naps' in an abandoned construction project, but it was just the first of many.

In the years that followed, Richard was arrested for almost every misdemeanour that the local police could come up with. His face was known, and whenever some petty crime had been committed, all that they had to do was roll around the abandoned houses until they spotted him drinking or popping back handfuls of his ill-gotten gains. His record of crimes grew longer with each passing day — the only real growth that was happening in the boy's life. He still attended school sporadically at his mother's request. Although he had lost a great deal of respect for her after her marriage to Carl, she still had a hold over him that was the envy of many of the other parents about town. If they ever had trouble with the young thug, all that it took was a word to his mother before he came around shamefaced to apologise. His academic career was not improved by liquor, and he was forced to repeat the eighth grade, in no small part because his terror of public speaking had come to a head as the girls in his class began to develop into their womanhood. The internal tension that had always surrounded his dealings with women came to a fever pitch when the fresh flush of teenage hormones was added into the mix. He went from loathing and resenting their attention to desperately craving it, for reasons that he still didn't have any rational reason for. He would follow the girls around, staring, but any attempt to engage him in conversation would set him off running, his face beet red with embarrassment.

At the same time that he was becoming more fixated on girls, his body seemed to rebel, flooding his face with acne. The unsanitary living conditions of his home, his terrible diet, and some bad luck with genetics resulted in his whole face being covered in pimples and boils throughout most of his teenage years. Even in the aftermath, when things began to improve for his face, he was permanently disfigured with pockmarks all over his cheeks.

Even interactions with his sister at home were becoming difficult for him. In the flea-ridden apartment, there was very little in the way of privacy, and he found himself unwillingly fascinated with Carolyn. He didn't have the distance of social barriers to keep him away from her, and whatever morality that might've restrained his interest was knocked out of him with the hammer blow years before. He never acted on any of the confusing impulses that being in close proximity to his teenage sister was rousing in him. His fear of the opposite sex was still sufficient to curb action, but the growing tension meant that even the one social outlet that he'd always enjoyed was now gone.

In the autumn of 1957, Richard started his first year at Crozier Technical High School in Dallas. It should've been a fresh start for the boy, a chance to mingle with children his own age who weren't already privy to his odd reputation, but instead, it was another nail in the coffin of him ever living a normal life. While the junior high had been happy to bounce the boy along from grade to grade if he showed even the vaguest aptitude, the high school was considerably stricter in their grading standards. By the end of his first year of studies, Richard had utterly failed every single class that the school had to offer. Rather than return to repeat the experience for a second time, the 16-year-old loner parted ways with education and set out into the world to make his fortune.

What followed was a cluster of arrests for various petty thefts, arrests for drunk and disorderly behaviour, arrests for possession of drugs, and a developing habit of the local police to swing by his house whenever any crime had been committed, just on the off chance that it was one of his. The moment that he was in the interrogation room, he told the police everything that they wanted to know. It was as though he didn't know that he was meant to lie about his illegal activities. He seemed almost relieved to have someone to speak to.

For three years, Richard lingered around the city of Dallas, creating trouble for himself and anybody that crossed his path, officially still living with his stepfather and Mary but mostly spending his days and nights out on the streets, looking for the next moment of relief from the constant tension that seemed to stalk his every waking moment.

With any other boy, it might've been said that he fell in with a bad crowd, but the truth was, Richard was the poison seed planted in any social group foolish enough to accept him. Even among the other petty criminals he was quietly despised, and the junkies and alcoholics of Dallas weren't the kindest at the best of times. Still, somebody must have liked him for a little while, because during those three years, someone put in the time and effort to tattoo the whole length of his forearm with the words, 'Born to Raise Hell'.

Richard was on a trajectory of self-destruction, and if nothing had changed during those three years, it's likely that his criminal career would've come to nothing more than petty theft and an early death in the cold embrace of hard drugs. But the changes that'd come over the boy hadn't gone entirely unnoticed. His mother had despaired, and his now ignored sister had pleaded with him to get his life in order. Neither of them had the power to bring him home, though. In the middle of that family, there was still a festering wound that wouldn't heal, and its name was Carl Lindberg.

In a strange twist of fate, it was actually Carl who saved Richard from an ignominious end, although, of course, it wasn't intentional. Carl had become increasingly disenchanted with his new wife and the family she brought along with her, in particular, the young brute that she was raising in Richard. He could still vividly remember the day back in Santo when a little boy swung a hammer at his face with murder in his eyes. Now that boy had grown up into a hateful young man, skinny but ridged with wiry muscles. If it came to a fight, he was no longer sure that he'd win, and if it came down to a brawl that he lost, he wasn't sure that he even had the moral high ground. He'd been the one to put the boy down all these years, to tell him he was worthless and useless. It was so obvious where the blame for Richard's outlook on life should lie that Carl couldn't even begin to deny it.

Carl started to spend more and more time away from home, ostensibly working but really just drinking and whoring his way around every city he could feasibly sell an insurance policy in. He vanished for weeks, then months at a time, before finally settling into a new life in California with some other young mother who was stupid enough to open her door to him. The more that he was away, the more that Richard came home at night, and when Carl vanished for the last time with nothing more than a postcard from California, Richard abandoned his street life entirely, to return to the fold as if nothing had happened in the intervening years.

He became the man of the house with Carl gone, and he shouldered the financial burden of caring for his family. The day after the postcard arrived, he marched himself down to the 7Up bottling factory and demanded a job. He had no standards and no compunctions, so they set him to work doing the kind of hard manual labour that had shaped his real father's life. It paid poorly, but it paid better than petty theft and alcoholism, and when his supervisors saw the boy's determination to do well, he found himself gradually shuffled into less arduous tasks for long periods of overtime. He was bringing home less pay than Carl had, but he wasn't drinking half of it before he even got to the front door. If anything, it seemed like the family's dire fortunes had been reversed by the removal of the parasitic stepfather who'd latched onto them. If Mary wept alone in her marriage bed at night, that was no business of her children.

Freed of Carl's oppressive presence, their whitewashed shack in East Dallas became something like a home again — someplace that neither Mary nor Carolyn had to be ashamed to bring friends back to. For all that Richard was a social pariah, Carolyn more than made up for his failings. She had been a social butterfly all the way through high school, doing well in her classes and drawing the attention of a great many suitors. With the house finally in some sort of order, she had the courage to bring one of them home to meet her mother.

Richard lurched in at the midpoint of dinner to find another man sitting in his seat by the kitchen table. But while he might have feared and loathed Carl for taking his father's place, he was glad to see someone else taking his place in his sister's affections. His discomfort and confusion around her had only grown through the years, and her physical displays of affection since he'd started setting his life in order had left him disturbed. To a normal brother, a kiss on the cheek or a brief hug as thanks wouldn't have warranted any concern, but for the intensely repressed Richard, they reminded him of the uncomfortable reality that his desires could never be sated. If she had some new boyfriend to shower all of her affection on, that was all the better for Richard. He could use the space.

For a while, there was something very much like peace in their home. Richard worked odd hours, taking whatever overtime he could to support the family. But with his newfound desire for silence, he moved in and out of the Lindberg women's lives like a ghost, anyway. He was present in the house sometimes, but it made little difference to the day-to-day running of things. Without him, everything would have fallen into poverty and disarray, but without any ability to communicate nor any desire to assert his control over the family the way that the previous 'men of the house' had insisted on, he was soon taken for granted.

This proved to be a mistake for Mary, at least. When she was too dismissive of Richard during a family discussion, he turned his fists on her readily. He'd been getting into bar brawls since he was tall enough to get inside, and while he seemed placid on the outside, he was still full of rage, most often directed to the women around him whom he considered to be treacherous and unworthy of the kind of treatment that they seemed to expect from him. His mother ended up with both of her eyes blackened, and the whole family developed a newfound respect for the quiet young man's opinions when he chose to voice them. The police weren't called, but Mary did have to visit a doctor later in the week when it seemed that Richard had broken her cheekbone, creating an official record of this first explosion of violence towards women.

Richard's drinking habit had become inconsistent since he took on the job at the bottling factory, but he still indulged more than was healthy. He suffered from excruciating headaches, which he would use liquor to self-medicate against. The hammer injury from his youth had caused permanent damage to the structure of his brain, compromising the part that managed impulse control and emotion, resulting in odd connections forming as the damage healed. It was likely the misfiring of neurons in his damaged brain that led to the pain that he suffered, something that consuming alcohol would have exacerbated rather than helping to numb. He had headaches because he drank, and he drank because he had headaches. If he came home smelling of whiskey, then Carolyn and Mary knew to steer well clear of him. He had never even considered hurting his sister — she was still perfect and pure in his eyes — but that didn't mean that she couldn't accidentally launch him into one of the furious rants that characterised his dark moods.

He'd been drinking when he assaulted his mother, and neither of the women wanted to see that event repeated. Strangely, it seemed to have frightened Carolyn more than Mary. Mary had seen violence and hatred in Richard all of his life. She'd recognised the moment when he no longer had any respect left for her after she'd married Carl and known that some sort of confrontation was inevitable. She hadn't expected him to speak with his fists, but she suspected that it was no worse than she deserved. Carolyn, on the other hand, had only ever seen the best of Richard. She'd always been the recipient of all his kindness and affection, shielded from any hint of the darkness inside him. Richard and his mother had both made a conscious effort to keep it from her. It was one of the few areas in his life where Richard seemed to be capable of maintaining any sort of restraint.

Despite this small disruption to the peace of the household, Carolyn's courtship continued, and more often than not, Richard would come home to the sounds of laughter in the house. There were smiles on his mother and sister's faces, and after the initial discomfort that the lanky and quiet Richard had caused, his soon-to-be brother-in-law accepted him as an oddball with a good heart. Even after Carolyn married, she and her new husband stayed on in the house in East Dallas, along with Richard and his mother. With the extra money coming in from another working man, things went from strained to altogether comfortable. Life was drastically improving for the Lindberg family, and it was about to get even better for Richard.

There were few things that could entice Richard out of the house when he didn't have to be working, beyond the eternal call of liquor, but one of the few events on the calendar that could get him out among the people that made him so uncomfortable was the Texas State Fair that took place every October. The fair was timed perfectly, just when the weather was starting to cool enough that he didn't mind being outside all day but before the rains swept through. The whole extended family rose with dawn and drove for an hour to arrive at the big open field that had been filled to bursting with rides, bandstands, coconut shies, shooting contests and tents. It was on the long thoroughfare, surrounded by sizzling funnel-cakes on one side and the kind of raucous laughter that usually made Richard cringe — assuming he was the butt of a joke — that he first laid eyes on the woman that would be his wife.

The Madonna

In 1961, Richard was 20 years old. Shirley Annette Malone was 15. She was attending the fair with her parents, and perhaps the fact that Richard was there with his mother, or it was his painful shyness, convinced her that he was similarly young. It's fair to say that Richard's sexual awakening was arrested when he was about Shirley's age, and he started to notice the girls in his class, and his household, more often. His growing attraction had to be stomped out for him to maintain his view of women as perfect and pure. Between his religious upbringing and his observations of the sexual world — mostly horrifying glimpses of his mother in congress with the stepfather that he hated — it was hardly surprising that his opinions on the matter were a little bit warped. What is surprising is that he had enough restraint to control his urges and enough respect for the 'pure' women that he lusted after to try to redirect the trajectory that his hormones had set him on.

Shirley was the first texception to the life of solitude that he'd set himself up for, a girl that he was so smitten with that he forgot all about his own internal conflict, at least for a while. She had wavy blonde hair, just like Carolyn, and the beginnings of a woman's body, just like Carolyn had when he'd pushed her away.

Whatever it was about Shirley, something in her pubescent appearance overpowered his usual ability to recognise an external danger to his mental balance.

The two of them spent the day together with the blessing of both sets of parents, who thought that the budding romance between their shy children was adorable rather than a cause for concern. The couple wandered the fairground hand in hand until the sun came down, and when they parted ways to go home with their respective families, it was with a promise that they'd see each other again soon. As it turned out, she was another resident of Dallas, albeit a slightly nicer neighbourhood, so the couple made arrangements to meet up once they were back in the city. When they went their separate ways, it was with big smiles on their faces.

Back in the city, and away from the watchful eyes of chaperones, the relationship progressed rapidly. With no real idea of what dating was meant to be like, and a desire to prove to Shirley that he was a mature adult and not the man-child everyone else saw, Richard took her out drinking about town. After visiting a few of his favourite spots, they discovered that their inhibitions, which had been barely present to start with, seemed to have dissolved in the alcohol. He'd already regressed to his teenage habit of day drinking, so it seemed only natural that he should follow it up by heading to a partially constructed house for a 'lie down'.

They would go out for a drink and a lie down several times over the following weeks. Richard had a whole lifetime of repressed sexual energy to let out, and Shirley was still suffering from a child's delusions of what romance could be. She thought that they were in love. So did Richard, for that matter. He had no basis for comparison, and he truly seemed to believe that his lust finally finding an outlet was the same thing. His image of Shirley still wasn't shattered — not yet. He could justify the things that they did together as innocent. He could pretend that it was the liquor that made her take off her clothes and lie under him as he rutted like an animal. He could take the blame on himself, pretend that he was the evil one, letting his wicked impulses drive him to take her against her will. As long as it was a secret between just the two of them, he never had to confront the reality of the situation. Shirley was happy. He was happy, too, when he wasn't having to leap through mental acrobatics to justify why Shirley was happy. Those three weeks, when they were together, were the happiest in Richard's life. He had it all — a job he excelled at, a family that cared for him, a perfect pure virgin girlfriend, and all the sex he'd been craving for years. Of course, it couldn't last.

When they met up for their latest date, Shirley declined a trip to the bars of town, instead asking Richard to take her somewhere quiet so they could talk. Neither one of them had anything beyond the most basic sex education. They knew how to perform the act, but their understanding of the consequences was hazy, at best. Even so, from talking with friends and extended family, Shirley had managed to piece the truth together. After just three weeks of their being together, she was pregnant.

Now there was undeniable proof of what the two of them had been doing in the dark, and Richard's perfect little bubble started to burst. When they'd been alone, it was easy for him to control his view of Shirley as pure, perfect and untainted, but now, everyone was going to see her. Everyone was going to know that she was nothing more than a whore.

They announced their news to the respective families, whose responses were pretty stereotypical of the time. Both sides immediately agreed that the young couple should get married as quickly as possible, preferably before Shirley started to give any indication that she was pregnant. Arrangements were hastily made, and within a few months, the couple were wed in a cheap ceremony with no questions asked.

This was a chance for Richard to start over fresh. He'd been rebuilding his life, step by step, ever since Carl left, and now it seemed he was moving on with his life instead of lingering in the shadows at the periphery of the lives of others. He changed his name at the same time as Shirley, scrubbing all hint of Carl from his life and doing due homage to his beloved, deceased father. He became Richard Speck and his wife, Shirley Speck.

While there were no threats made and there was a general air of goodwill between the two families, the event was still unmistakably a shotgun wedding. Shirley's family fully expected Richard to make the situation right and to care for both mother and baby entirely without their assistance.

The truly bizarre thing is that for the first time in his life, Richard was in a situation where he absolutely could've made good on those promises. His job paid well enough, he had the support of his mother and younger sister, and despite all of the pressures being exerted on them, his relationship with Shirley was considerably more solid than could be expected. She moved into the house that he shared with his mother and sister's burgeoning family, and Mary immediately took the young girl under her wing, teaching her how to do all the things that her mother had not, setting her to some light work around the house so that she could feel like she was earning her keep. Richard returned to work with a renewed vigour. He had a new mouth to feed, and it was eating for two, so he took on any shifts that came his way, insulating the family coffers as much as possible before the baby arrived. Everything was still on course to work out for the newly made Speck family, if he could've just kept his internal conflicts under control.

One night, on his return from work, he found that Shirley had already gone to bed without him. He ate the cool leftovers of the family meal at the kitchen table in sullen silence then retreated to his bedroom as soon as they were finished. Shirley was lying asleep in their bed, the beginnings of her pregnancy bump already starting to show. Before his very eyes, it seemed that her body was transforming, mutating from the beautiful slender virgin that he'd always wanted into just another bloated whore. To his disgust, he found himself aroused at the sight of her, at the new curves and swellings that he knew were a sign of her corruption. He stripped out of his clothes and climbed on top of her, and it was only the sudden crushing weight of him on top of her that finally caused Shirley to stir. 'Not tonight, sweetheart'.

She'd never said no to him before. Not ever. It was all that it took to push him over the edge. He pinned her to the bed by her wrists and forced his way between her thighs. She tried to struggle free, yelping, 'The baby!'

If she thought that the baby would protect her from his fury, she was sadly mistaken. She was holding it up like a talisman of innocence, but to Richard, it was just evidence that she was a whore. A filthy whore who had sex, got pregnant and latched onto him like a tick, swelling larger and larger with every passing day as he felt all his strength ebbing away. Now this whore was saying no to him. The one thing that whores were good for, and she was telling him he couldn't have it? To hell with that! He hit her again and again, long after she'd stopped resisting, long after she'd spread her legs and he'd forced himself inside, a punctuation to every thrust.

When it was all over, she lay there, shocked and numb until he rolled her back onto her side of the bed and fell asleep as if it was the most natural thing in the world. The next morning, after she'd lain awake all night, shuddering in pain and disgust, he acted as if nothing had happened. In his mind, nothing had. Everything in the world was as it should be.

She resisted him often from that day forward, refusing all of his advances and doing her best to stay in the company of the rest of his family to thwart his attempts to get her into bed. He'd always known that his lust was a poison, and now the burgeoning relationship with his wife was beginning to sicken as a result of it. All of the affection that he'd felt for Shirley withered in the face of her refusal to meet his nightly demands, and the more that she refused him, the more that he beat her and forced himself upon her. His feelings towards her might've been complicated, but

Shirley's couldn't have been simpler — she loathed him. He'd gone from being the man she loved to her jailor and tormentor, and if she could've left right then and there she would have, but she had nowhere to go. Her family wouldn't take her back. She had no money of her own. Her only support in the world was Mary and Carolyn, and they were bound to Richard financially just as surely as she was.

That tie would begin to wither in the coming months as his pay began to dwindle. He'd stopped seeking out extra shifts. Some days he would be late to work, and some days he wouldn't show up at all. His reputation in the bottling plant plummeted, but he couldn't bring himself to care. Along with the return of his violent temper and his misery, the headaches had resurfaced, more regular and vicious than ever before. He began drinking daily to try and curb the worst of his suffering, and the more that he drank, the crueller he became towards his young wife. When the booze didn't work, he turned to pills, and when the pills didn't work, he started to mix and match, desperate for some relief from the constant turmoil that haunted him. He showed up to work less and less; he came home less and less. In some ways, it was a relief for the rest of the family, but the financial strain for Carolyn's husband was insurmountable. He couldn't afford to keep two wives, a mother-in-law and himself. They were on the borderline of destitution once more. Richard took to sleeping off his binges in houses that were under construction, and if it crossed his mind that his marriage was falling apart in the same place that it had been haphazardly slapped together, then he never spoke about it.

The police became familiar with Richard again but for a new variety of crimes. Where before he'd been a boy trying to navigate an adult world of addicts and dealers, he was now an adult with cash to spend, fully immersed in the alcoholic subculture of Texas. He would get into bar fights with regularity, desperate for some way to vent his foul mood on others and just looking for any excuse to start a brawl. When the attention of the police grew too heavy a burden to bear, he would hop freight trains with the homeless addicts to travel to nearby towns where he wasn't so well-known to the law. He'd drink until he woke up in the town's drunk tank or passed out in an alleyway, only to wander home days later reeking of his own filth.

The closer that it came to the baby's due date, the more he drank. His job at the bottling plant was no longer waiting for him when he sobered up, and he had to go further and further afield to find a barman foolish enough to let him run up a tab. Back at home, Shirley had passed her breaking point. There was no good reason for her to continue lingering in poverty with the threat of Richard's return hanging over her when she could just as easily live in poverty somewhere safe. Still, some part of her clung to the romantic idea that the Richard she once knew was still inside the monster somewhere and that when the baby came, he would put aside all of this foolishness and come to his senses.

She held onto that dim hope up until the final moments of her labour. Even as she was pushing their daughter out, her eyes kept on turning towards the door, hoping against all evidence that Richard would appear and make everything right again. He did not, and he could not. Robbie Lynn Speck was born on the fifth of July, 1962, with her father nowhere to be found.

Days before, he had gone off on another bender, this time finding himself in McKinney, Texas. While he diligently worked his way through a bar's stock of the very worst whiskey, somebody did something to offend him. It may have been nothing more than a glance. It didn't take much to set Richard off in those days. Sadly, nobody was sober enough to recall exactly what set the incident off. But it ended in a bar brawl that resulted in another man being hospitalised and Richard being confined to a cell for 22 days for disturbing the peace.

When he was finally released and limped home, Shirley was not there waiting for him. His sister was there, his mother, too, but not his wife nor his daughter. He tried to work over the family for information, but fresh out of prison, he was far from his physical prime. His brother-in-law was hovering in the background, just waiting for his hollow threats and bellowing to go further, but for all of his myriad flaws, Richard wasn't stupid enough to pick a fight he couldn't win. Not sober, anyway.

He found out about Robbie Lynn on the first day, and he also found out how it felt to be held in absolute contempt by the women who meant the most to him in the world. Shirley might've degenerated into whoredom in his eyes, but his mother and sister were still pinnacles of virginal perfection. They'd pitied him before, even been angry at him, but this was the first time that he'd truly believed that they might stop loving him. He couldn't bear it. The weight of guilt that they brought to bear against him drove him, ever so briefly, back onto the straight and narrow. He quit drinking and swore to prove his worth to Shirley — and to the family — and win her back. He didn't succeed.

While he managed to secure a job at the bottling plant after a great deal of tooth-grinding grovelling, he didn't last for long. His headaches and temper continued to present a problem, and even when he did show up to work, he was often too drunk to do much more than linger around the warehouse picking fights with the other workers. He knew that he was on the way out. The same people who'd once looked at him with pride beaming from their faces now couldn't meet his eye. It was just a matter of time until they found some excuse to lay him off, and he still didn't have enough cash to get his own place and entice Shirley back to him.

He needed to make all of the money that he could out of the 7Up plant fast before they could get rid of him, so in July of 1963, he made his move. Sadly, his awareness of the moods of others, finely honed after years in a household with an abusive stepfather, was not sufficient to protect him from the consequences of the stupid decisions that were soon to follow.

All of the employees' cheques were slipped into a pigeonhole for them to collect at the end of the week. In a moment of madness, Richard grabbed his own and a co-worker's at the same time. The other cheque was only for $44 when he finally slipped it out of the envelope, but by now, he'd already committed to his course of action. Returning the cheque and pretending that he'd picked it up by mistake didn't even cross his mind. If he wanted his baby, he needed money. If he wanted money, he'd have to cash this cheque. Despite all of his academic failings, Richard had learned how to write — and how to write neatly in cursive — at least well enough to passably forge a signature.

The cheque was cashed, and his fate was sealed. He stewed in his room at home throughout all of that Saturday, just waiting for the knock of the police on the door, but it never came. Somehow, he'd gotten away with a crime for the first time in his life. By Sunday morning, he was convinced that his luck had finally changed. If he could commit crimes with impunity, there was a lot more money in the world than he'd thought of just a day ago. Over the course of the day, he scoped out local businesses and finally broke into a grocery store after the sun had set, to make off with all the cash in the register. A grand total of three dollars in change, since the place had been closed all day and cashed out for the weekend. He was furious at the pathetic haul that he'd risked so much for and decided to drown his sorrows in a beer, which he also lifted from the store along with a carton of cigarettes. He had himself a very lacklustre party that night, all alone in his room. If he'd known that it was his last night of freedom, he would likely have gone for something a little grander.

When Monday rolled around and he went to work, it was to face down his supervisor and a whole trade union's worth of warehouse workers, every one of them absolutely furious with him. He tried to feign ignorance, but he'd been seen lifting the brown envelope on Friday evening. He was laid off on the spot, and the police were waiting for him outside when he left the building. He didn't bother to run, instead, walking straight up to them with his wrists held out. He knew the drill by now. He was charged with fraud and for the burglary from the night, for which he slipped up and spoke about it as if the police already knew all of his crimes. He was tried and convicted of both the fraud and the burglary and sentenced to three years in prison. He was 21 years old.

The Loss

Richard was delivered from the courtroom to the Texas State Penitentiary in Huntsville, where he would spend the next year before he had any hope of parole. It wasn't his first time inside a prison, but it was certainly his longest sentence to date. Where before he'd been able to keep to himself and wait out the days, this time, he had to interact with his fellow prisoners in the long term, something he certainly wasn't equipped for. Between his bizarre home life, terror of attention and awkwardness with the opposite sex, his social skills had never had the opportunity to blossom, yet here, being able to safely navigate conversations, was the difference between life and death.

Once again, his strange empathy saved him. He was able to read his fellow prisoners quite easily, and thanks to his continuing headaches and the resultant fury, he was able to establish himself as a threatening presence, despite his youth. The combination of traits that had developed in response to his stepfather's abuse made him perfectly adapted for prison. He could prey on those weaker than him while still avoiding confrontation with those who were stronger.

He managed to make it through the first year of his sentence without any clashes with the guards, despite his open disdain for them and his repeated flagrant violations of the rules. As far as the guards were concerned, if they didn't have evidence of Richard beating on the weaker prisoners, it didn't happen. Nobody came forward, either, due to fear of Richard or just a general fear of reprisal if they gave information to the guards.

Despite all of this, Richard found his own niche within the prison, with something resembling friends. There was no shortage of addicts and junkies in the prison, and while Richard looked down on the proto-hippies, the more hardcore alcoholics and drug dealers were his people. Yet, despite the readily available drugs and liquor available in the prison, Richard mostly abstained. He had a new addiction now, a new obsession; his daughter.

'Born to Raise Hell' was emblazoned on one of his arms, but his needle-collecting friends in the prison were happy to decorate the other one with the words 'Robbie Lynn'. In a strange way, it was like he was trying to balance his desire for chaos and violence with his love for this one perfect and pure girl in his life. The one who could always maintain that perfection in his mind because the two of them still hadn't ever met. Throughout his whole prison stay, he kept his mind on Robbie Lynn and the life that he was going to make for them when he got out. If Shirley still factored into his thinking, he never mentioned her, except as a necessary accessory to his daughter.

With that one goal in mind, and a steady outlet for his more violent bullying impulses, he was able to pass through 16 months in Huntsville Penitentiary without any trouble, receiving commendations for his good behaviour when the time came for parole hearings. With the blessing of the prison's warden, Richard was released on 2 January 1965.

On his return home, Richard found that much had changed. Carolyn and her husband were expecting a baby, so they'd moved into their own place, leaving Mary completely alone with her youngest son. Without the buffer of their company, he soon found Mary's constant mothering to be smothering. On the positive side, without Carolyn and her husband there for moral support, Mary was a lot more susceptible to Richard's badgering demands for information about Shirley and his daughter. The news was not good.

During his prison stay, rumours had started circulating around town about the fate of Shirley and her daughter. There'd been a lot of fear that the poor girl would be driven to destitution by the cruel twists of fate that had landed her as a single mother. But with Richard out of the picture in prison, it seemed like she'd landed on her feet. Attitudes were changing, and while women's liberation would still take many years to surface, many men could look at the beautiful young woman and see her for what she was, not just the baby at her hip.

Shirley had lived alone for several months, struggling to get by on charitable contributions from the church, the Lindbergs and her mother, but it hadn't taken long before men came sniffing around. One man, in particular, seemed to be genuine in his affections, a young man known to Richard only as 'Mr Price'. Price had gone about courting Shirley in a very traditional manner before he realised the dire financial straits that she was in and started pushing their relationship forward at a much faster pace. If it weren't for Richard, it's likely that the two of them would already have been wed.

Mary expected Richard to be furious at this news, but if anything, it stripped him of a lot of his nervous energy. If Shirley was with another man, that gave him a sense of vindication. He'd always known that Shirley had left him to whore it up with other men. He'd always known that the fault was with her and not him, and this news just confirmed all of those suspicions. His worldview, which had been thrown into disarray by his marriage and his happiness, could now be reasserted without any inconvenience. Women were all whores. He was better than them.

Robbie Lynn became his sole fixation at that point. He may have talked a big game about murdering Shirley, bragging to his friends at the bar that the only reason he was still in Texas was to hunt her down and gut her like a pig, but he didn't make any active effort to go after her despite the ease with which he could've done so. In the eyes of the law, the two of them were still married, and even if they were separated, he would've had a legal claim to time with his daughter. Once again, Richard's lack of understanding of the mechanics of the real world crippled him in his pursuits.

He had a little money still saved from before he went to prison, but he began to drink his way through it at a rapid pace. The only real investment he made was in a 17-inch carving knife. His time bullying weaker prisoners had reminded him how much he used to enjoy menacing people in the plant with the box cutters that they provided to staff, and also reminded him of how much of a difference carrying a weapon could make to his ongoing survival in the rough-and-tumble world that he lived in. He wore the knife — really more of a short sword — tucked through his belt and covered by his jacket, but everyone in the bars he frequented knew that it was there, and he wasn't above brandishing it at the bartenders to get his way.

One week after his release from prison on parole, he set out to spend the last of his money in a few of his favourite dive bars. In the morning, he would be broke and hungover, but for one night, he just wanted to cut loose, relax and have a good time. He drank through the whole evening and into the early hours of the morning, but the release that he was seeking always seemed to be just out of reach. He'd never been truly content in all of his life, but there'd been times before Shirley when he'd been able to achieve a kind of peace, found right down at the bottom of a whiskey bottle — times when he could get so drunk that the screaming contradictions in his mind could be numbed into silence. Tonight, every sip of rotgut just seemed to make the noise louder, and it didn't take long for him to lock all of that raging turmoil onto a single target, Shirley. Before, the rage of betrayal had been subsumed by the vindication that he'd been feeling, but now that his worldview had settled back into its rigid form, he found that he was furious at her. Impotently furious. He had no way of getting to her. No way of getting his baby back from her. Reminiscing over old regrets is a common activity for alcoholics, but for Richard, the memories came with an emotional kick that remained overpowering despite the intervening years. She was his, and she'd up and left him while he was locked up.

At around two in the morning, he stormed out of the bar after trying and failing to start a fight several times. He was blind drunk, and whatever self-control he had was drowned in whiskey. A few streets from the bar, he found a woman trying to get into her car and rushed at her, brandishing his knife. In his eyes, this random woman was a symbol of everything wrong with the world. Out late at night on her own, to his mind, she was clearly a prostitute, one of the whores he was forever ranting about, and he wanted to punish her. More than punishment, he wanted to strip her of her beauty, hack away at the face that had made his breath catch when he first saw it. He wanted, above all else, to break the power that women had over him.

But then, he was shaken out of his fantasy by the shrill sound of her scream.

He fumbled the knife and nearly dropped it, suddenly face to face with the stark reality of what he'd planned to do. That, more than the night air, sobered him up in an instant. He opened his mouth to apologise, to make some excuse for his behaviour, but the truth was that there was no excuse — he'd come at that woman planning to murder and mutilate her. He'd lost control of himself completely for the first time in his life. As she continued to scream and the lights in nearby windows flicked on, Richard finally regained control of his body. He turned and ran for his life.

Just a few blocks away, the police intercepted him. As with every other time that he was questioned by the police, he made no attempt to lie. The testimony that he gave to them about why he'd done what he did was all that it took to convict him in court. The poor woman that he'd menaced didn't even have to show up to the trial. On top of the six months of outstanding time that he now had to serve for violating his parole, he was convicted of aggravated assault and sentenced to a further 16 months in prison.

After just one week of freedom, Richard was returned to Texas State Penitentiary. His old bunk hadn't even been reassigned yet, and he slipped back into his old routine almost casually. Given the size of the facility, most of the guards and prisoners didn't even realise that he'd left.

Throughout his sentence, he would brag incessantly about the revenge he was going to take on his wife, the cheating, baby-stealing whore of his nightmares personified. By the end of six months, everyone in the prison knew the girl's name and knew the fate that he had planned for her. They also knew that Richard had always talked a big game about the crimes he'd perpetrated and would go on to commit in the future. He was one of the curious subset of criminals who thought that their crimes made them better than other people — the people who brag about all of the women that they've raped or the men they've killed, like it's a game, and the more misery and destruction that they cause, the higher their score.

When the guards came to collect him from his cell only a few months into his sentence, Richard assumed it was because of these threats that he'd been bandying about. He imagined he was about to be dragged off and dressed down by the warden, warned that he wouldn't receive parole again if he kept it up. He certainly didn't expect to be released after only a fraction of his sentence was served. A mistake in the paperwork at the prison resulted in his being released early, at the end of his original sentence instead of his new one. It was a minor miracle for Richard, like fate had reached down and wiped his foolish mistake with the knife away.

On that fateful night, when he went after that woman, he'd lost control of himself in a way that scared even Richard. His temper had always been present, always providing him with the fire that he needed to get things done, but that had been the first time that rage had taken the reigns from reason. He never meant for it to happen again. If he was going to do bad things, it would be because he chose to do them, not because he was angry at the world.

He stepped off the prison bus in Dallas with a crooked smile on his face and a glint in his eye. He was going to find some balance in his life between the wildness that he loved and the stability that he required to maintain control of himself. When he set out to raise hell, he meant for every moment of it to be deliberate.

The Last Days of Dallas

After prison, Richard returned to his mother, but even she could see that something had changed in him. The rage that had always been barely contained beneath the surface hadn't disappeared, but he was channelling it into action in a way that he'd never known how to before. Within a week of his unexpected release, he'd secured a job for himself at Patterson Meat Company, driving one of their delivery trucks. The work was monotonous, and the pay was below par, primarily because it was well known to the staff that he was an ex-convict. The tattoos gave him away as much as his attitude, and they were aware that his options were limited.

To liven up his days, he would stop at several bars around town that were near to his drop-off points, but only one captured his affections, a rickety dive called Ginny's Lounge. Something in the bar's rustic décor seemed to remind him of a better time in his life, and the bartender and owner, Ginny, a woman who'd retired early from a career as a professional wrestler, captivated him. He'd never met a woman who was stronger than him before, and while it threw some of his assumptions about the world into question, he still spent hour after hour perched on a barstool watching the muscles shift beneath her clothes. His attentions were noticed and, if not reciprocated, then at least appreciated. Ginny was an older woman who'd suffered through an unpleasant divorce, and despite his pock-marked face, there was no denying that Richard had some strange charisma to him now that he had his temper in check. She flirted with him gently, like she was scared that he might run away.

Drinking throughout the day and driving a truck led to the inevitable sooner rather than later. Richard had a car accident just a few weeks into his new employment that put a massive scratch along the side of his truck. His employers were furious and threatened to dock his wages, but they never quite followed through on that threat — not that first time that he crashed, nor the second, nor any of the other times that he returned the truck damaged by some fender bender or another. Within three months of working at Patterson Meat Company, he managed to crash six times, yet still, they kept him on the payroll as if it were no problem at all. Indeed, he probably would have held on to that job forever if he'd just shown up to work each day. Sadly, his fixation on Ginny's Lounge soon outweighed his desire to work, and he started heading straight there in the mornings after he'd left his mother's company. If he noticed the marked similarity between his domineering mother and the powerful woman behind the bar, then he never commented upon it.

He lost his driving job soon after he started skipping out to spend his day in the bar, and without him having any income, Mary began to become concerned for the future of her youngest son. She was getting by all right thanks to the help that her other, more mature children, were sending along to her, along with a part-time job of her own, but it wasn't enough to support Richard, too. Not for any length of time, anyway. Still, every day he left the house with clockwork regularity, and when he came dawdling home, he was sober enough to walk straight, and he had a dreamy smile on his face.

Even after all of this time, Mary was incapable of letting him live his own life without interference. Even after he turned his fists and all of his spite on her through the years, she still saw him as a baby to be cared for and sheltered. It was with this mental image in mind that she followed him out of the house one morning, creeping along the streets behind him in her car until he arrived at Ginny's Lounge, to which she let out a sigh of dismay. Her boy had turned to drink yet again — not his first vice but certainly his most persistent. She crept into the cool dark of the bar, expecting to find him knocking back liquor with his usual determination. Instead, he was perched at the head of the bar, hanging on every word of the powerful-looking woman standing behind it. Mary didn't linger long, but what she saw convinced her that there was hope on the horizon rather than another wave of despair. Richard was smitten again, and by the kind of woman who looked like she'd stand up for herself and put him in his place. Someone who could knock all the nonsense out of his head if it looked like he was going to cause trouble. She came to the same conclusion as her son as she stared at the woman behind the bar. She was perfect.

A few days later, she raised the subject with Richard over dinner. He was in one of his sullen, silent moods, and his mother prying into his business yet again did nothing to help with that. He wasn't surprised that she knew about Ginny's Lounge or his fixation on Ginny herself. When he wasn't damning her as a vile whore in his mind, he still held onto the childlike belief that his mother saw all and knew all. Given the way she invaded his privacy, this belief may not have been entirely unfounded. She started the interrogation gently, asking about the new woman in her son's life, teasing out details, and finding out just how far along their relationship had gotten. She had already been making enquiries about town, and she already knew the exact angle of approach that she was going to make — she just wanted Richard to feel like the idea was his own.

With the careful and gradual application of pressure, she edged Richard out of her house and into Ginny's, using the best leverage that she had available to her at the time. Ginny had two kids and nobody to take care of them while she worked at the bar downstairs. If Richard could make himself seem like a decent enough father figure, or at least a viable free babysitter, then it seemed likely she would take him in. As much as he loathed his mother's intervention in his romantic overtures, Richard was starting to get desperate. He'd been hanging around Ginny's Lounge for months with no success. If he didn't get that woman into bed soon, he was worried he might explode.

The first time that he offered to babysit Ginny's kids, he expected trouble. He couldn't think of any world in which a man would offer to watch kids that weren't his, and he expected to be rebuffed so badly that his months of flirtation would fall apart in moments. Instead, he was overwhelmed with Ginny's gratitude. She wrapped him up in a hug, squeezing him with her strong arms and filling him with even more mixed feelings than before. That same night, he sat up in her apartment drinking alone, listening for any sound from the kids that were already asleep by the time that he arrived. They didn't stir. He wouldn't even meet them until the following morning. He sat and stared into space, and he drank until the early hours of the morning when Ginny came up the back stairs and let herself in. She slumped onto the couch beside him, exhausted from a long night of work and slid into his arms, without him even having to say a word. She took him to bed with her that night and every night afterwards when he was sitting there waiting for her. He became a part of her routine. His warm body in her bed was appreciated as much as the money she was saving on a babysitter every night.

Richard found his lust fulfilled for no more a price than a few hours of wasted time each night when he would've just been lounging around and drinking at home anyway. Here, he didn't have his mother staring at him all the time, and he didn't have to buy his own beer. Still, the shadow of his mother's influence hung over the whole thing. He couldn't shake the suspicion that this was exactly what she wanted, him gone from her life, him sitting here bored. His fixation on Ginny hadn't abated, but it was clear that her interest in him was more practical than romantic, and he missed the days when Shirley had mooned after him with words of love on her lips. Sex with Shirley had been evil and sordid, but it had always been fuelled by their shared passion for one another. With Ginny, he half expected her to pat him on the back and tell him 'well done' when it was all over. He was a house-pet more than a man in Ginny's life, and his ego couldn't tolerate it.

He began to sneak down to the bar later in the evening to have a drink or two in the company of his old crowd. Ginny didn't like it, but he was usually quite brief before he returned to his duties upstairs, so she let it slide. She reasoned that not much could happen in the half-hour he was downstairs, that he was just missing the bar scene where he'd spent all his time before he met her. She made excuses for him, just like every other woman in his life had, and it ended as well for her as it had all of them.

In January of 1966, Shirley officially filed for divorce. Despite their long separation and the fact that he'd been shacked up with another woman for several months now, it was still enough to send Richard into a blind rage. How dare she file for divorce? He was her husband; she was his property. As always, he directed that rage inwards and fed it into his twisted view on women. They were all whores, just waiting for the opportunity to step out on their man, just waiting for any excuse to cheat. He started to linger down in the bar for longer and longer each night, watching Ginny instead of drinking. More specifically, watching the way that she flirted with her patrons for tips. All of his suspicions seemed to be playing out before his very eyes.

When he saw her fingers linger in one man's hand for a moment too long as she handed him his change, Richard flew into a fury. He rushed across the room and grabbed the man by his collar, flinging him to the ground. In the distance, he could hear Ginny screaming his name, but it was too far away to matter. All that he could feel was the thunder of his own heartbeat. His blood roared in his ears; his hands moved with a speed and grace he didn't think he'd be capable of matching in sanity. As the man tried to rise, Richard beat him down. When he lashed out a foot and set Richard staggering, he found his balance without even trying, and when the man rose up to bull rush him in a classic American-football tackle, the knife was in Richard's hand without his ever drawing it. Blood splashed on the floorboards, and the man's friends finally intervened, not daring to risk coming in reach of the bug-eyed fury of Richard but grabbing their buddy and dragging him away before anything worse could happen. They got him out into the street, and Richard could already hear sirens. He turned with the knife in his hand to slit the throat of whichever coward had called the cops on him, and there was Ginny by the payphone, staring at him like she'd never seen him before. This man, whom she'd trusted to take care of her children. This man, whom she'd welcomed into her home and her bed. This man, who now had blood splattered across him and was staring back at her with the same lost little boy eyes that had endeared him to her in the first place. He dropped the knife as the rush of anger washed away in shame, and she ran right by him to go meet the ambulance outside. She would never talk to him again.

Since it was a stabbing, the police arrived just behind the ambulance, and with one brief look at Richard lurking by the side of the bar, they knew they had their perpetrator. He was dragged off to questioning, and for the first time, his emotional state was actually given some consideration by the police. Every other arrest had been as a result of his alcoholism or drugs, for petty crimes and robberies to fund those addictions. This was the first crime of passion that the Dallas police had ever seen Richard commit, and they had some sympathy for him. He saw some other man flirting with his girl, they got into a fight, and somebody got hurt. That wasn't a crime in the eyes of most of the men on the force. They probably wouldn't have even pushed for him to serve jail time.

Unfortunately, with his previous criminal record, there was no other outcome for a man like Richard when he was charged with aggravated assault. Worse yet, if he was put back into the system, then it was likely his outstanding prison time would be discovered. He would probably even have other charges added on for 'escaping' ahead of his release date, thanks to the administrative error. Any criminal charge, large or small, would have been enough to lock him up, potentially for a decade.

That was when his overbearing mother showed up to court with a cheap lawyer by her side. The lawyer presented legal arguments while Mary wheedled incessantly at the district attorney until finally, they came to an agreement. Richard would plead guilty to the misdemeanour of creating a public disturbance, and in exchange, the charge of aggravated assault would be dropped. It was an incredibly sweet deal, fuelled by a great deal of kindness and understanding for Richard's situation on all sides. He had nothing but contempt for it. He took the plea, received a $10 fine for his actions, and then promptly refused to pay it.

In lieu of payment, the court charged him with three days of imprisonment in the local jail. Compared to the prison where he'd spent so many years, it was nothing. It was more comfortable than the home where he'd grown up and more comfortable than the street he would've been dumped onto now that he was out of Ginny's house, by far. Everyone knew him there — he was an old familiar face — and the pressures that plagued him in his life outside faded into insignificance. In jail, nobody expected him to be anything more or less than what he so obviously was.

He returned home to his mother after his three days were through, and the weight of her attention began to grind him down. She wanted him gone. He had no doubt about that now. The vicious, gibbering part of his brain said that she wanted him out of the way so she could whore around with whatever men she wanted, but the reality remained the same as always. She wanted her son to start his own life and give what was left of her life back.

He didn't attempt to go back to Ginny's Lounge. He had no idea what sort of welcome was waiting for him there, and he didn't fancy testing his strength or his fury against the woman who'd so effortlessly rolled him around a bed.

With the constant niggling demand of his mother in his mind, he started finding work around town, odd jobs that could put a little cash in his pocket, and cover his bar tab in the other places around town. Nobody wanted to take him on in the long term, but his strength and work ethic were admirable while they lasted. He would work himself to exhaustion until he got that first paycheque, then he'd vanish to spend it, resulting in a pretty fair belief that he was unreliable. He still drank and took drugs as frequently as possible, but as his mother became more and more overbearing, acting as if she owned his life now that she'd saved him from years in jail, he now had another reason for wanting money. The wants of the man and mother had finally aligned — they both wanted him in his own place, well away from her.

The money didn't come in fast enough for Richard's liking, and every night that he had to go home to his mother's henpecking was another nail in the coffin of his fleeting moments of drunken happiness. Just as he had when he thought that he could recapture his wife and daughter, he began to grow desperate for money and ever-more foolish with it, too. On an impulse, he decided that he needed a car of his own. If he had a car, then he could leave town, go somewhere else and start over. He could do odd jobs for people, anywhere. There was nothing keeping him in Dallas except bad memories. Gathering up all that he'd managed to save, Richard trawled the bars of Dallas looking for somebody with an old car for sale.

On 5 March 1966, he finally found something he could afford — a 12-year-old rust bucket that probably wouldn't make it across town, let alone all the way to whatever distant city

Richard imagined a new life for himself in. Almost immediately, he was overwhelmed with buyer's remorse. All the money that he'd been saving for months had just vanished in an instant, and all he had to show for it was a car and his name on some papers. When he thought about how much oblivion that same cash could've bought him, it brought him close to tears. He needed the money back, right now. The seller had sensibly made himself scarce, so Richard turned to his usual panic position when he needed cash fast — burglary of a local store.

He waited until the next day, drove up to the closed shop and broke in the same way as he had the last one. He checked the till out of habit more than expectation, pocketed the change and then filled his arms up with cartons of cigarettes. Going back and forth, he managed to pilfer seventy cartons in all. He knew from years of watching his mother cutting deals for cheap cigarettes from the local roughs that there was good money in selling these along. He just didn't know how to get from where he was to that money. Luckily, some of the locals, finding that the shop was shut, were quick to unburden him of a few packs of cigarettes at a hefty discount over what they'd usually have paid. They came back with friends, and before long, Richard was doing a roaring trade out of the back of his car. He made more selling his stolen cigarettes in that one night than he had in all of his days doing odd jobs. But as the night drew down and his customers became more and more scarce, he was left alone with his thoughts, and despite how impulsive his actions had been so far, he wasn't stupid. Every one of the people who'd bought from him tonight was a potential witness, as were all the other people who'd been passing by. The moment that somebody realised that the shop had been broken into, somebody would be describing him parked outside, selling the stolen goods along. He was kicking himself for his impulsive behaviour for the second time in as many days. When it was full dark, he did the only thing that made sense to get some distance — he took the cash and abandoned his car in the parking lot.

An arrest warrant was issued for him on the eighth of March. He had abandoned the car with the freshly signed paperwork still in the glovebox, and it had taken all of five minutes for the police to look up the original owner and confirm that it'd been sold along to Richard. He'd spent the night camped out in a partially constructed house on the outskirts of town, shivering in the dark and hoping that, this time, just for once, he'd gotten away with something. It just wasn't his night.

By the time he returned home after lying low for a day, it was midmorning, and his mother was already on the verge of hysterics. Mary grabbed her son by the shoulders and dragged him out of sight of the street the moment he came through the door. She probably would have beaten him, but the last time she'd raised a hand to him, he'd given her a crack in the jaw that she wouldn't soon forget. She'd already been warned by friends that the police were looking for him again, and there was nothing that she could do to save him this time. If they caught him, this would be his forty-second arrest in Dallas. There was no possibility of parole or pleas, not with so many witnesses and so much evidence against him already in the pocket of the police. He would be going back to jail, and with this many repeat offences, he would be going back for 10 years or more.

Richard was on the edge of despair with nobody to turn to. He'd alienated and cursed everyone that might help him. Everybody except for his beloved sister, Carolyn. She showed up in her husband's car, unannounced, and manhandled Richard out of the house before the police could arrive to arrest him. She drove him across town to the bus station and slipped him some cash for a cross-country ticket to the dubious safety of Chicago. He hadn't spoken to her properly in years. He had no idea how to thank her. She pressed a kiss to his forehead in silence then shoved him out of the car. His time in Dallas was done.

You Can Never Go Home

In Chicago, Richard was collected from the bus station by his sister, Martha. She was so much older than him that the two had barely spoken in their entire lives. By the time that he was old enough to even comprehend the world around him, she'd already drifted out of the family home and into the adult world. Throughout his childhood, he caught only brief glimpses of her when she visited, almost always clad in the pristine white uniform of a student nurse. She'd met her husband, Gene Thornton, when he was on shore leave from the U.S. Navy. When he came out of the forces, she'd entered the kind of retirement so many women in those days took; the kind that involved marriage and children.

Gene didn't take to Richard the way that Martha had. In his eyes, the man was a waste of skin. He didn't have a job, he did nothing to contribute to society, and he really didn't like the way that the man eyed his teenaged daughters. He never outright told Richard to leave, but almost as soon as he arrived, Gene started grilling him on his plans for his next move. The future seemed like a safer topic for her husband to delve into than the past, so Martha did nothing to chide him. They both knew that Richard had been in some sort of trouble down in Dallas, but they didn't know the depth of it. There'd been some talk in the family about drink, drugs, a bad divorce, and even some jail time, but prying open that can of worms seemed like it would cause more trouble than it was worth. As long as he didn't cause any trouble while he was under their roof, Richard could keep his cards close to his chest.

The badgering to move on began to grate at Richard after only a couple of days in Chicago, and with the watchful eye of Gene constantly on him, he barely even got to have a drink before he was dragged back to their house for a family dinner and an early night, every night. In Martha, he saw a chance to form the kind of maternal relationship that he'd always wanted, but he had just enough self-awareness to recognise that he couldn't form that relationship just yet. He wanted her to love him with a desperation that was quite unsettling to him, and he understood that if he revealed too much of the truth about himself, he was liable to scare her off permanently. Her husband clearly wanted him out, and he needed some distance so that he didn't ruin this second chance at a decent relationship with a mother figure.

It was agreed between the three of them that he would move back to Monmouth, Illinois, where some of the family were still lingering and where he might have more support than Martha alone could offer him. It would be a chance to start his life over and get it right this time, going back to the place where he'd once lived in the shadow of his real father, walking down a path towards being a decent man. The symbolism wasn't lost on Richard, and he readily agreed to the plan, particularly when a quick ring around the family and a few friends secured him a job in Monmouth as soon as he could get there. He packed up his single suitcase, wished Martha a tearful goodbye, and climbed onto another Greyhound bus that same night.

On arrival in Monmouth, Richard was picked up by what was now his eldest brother, Howard, and driven to his job. Howard had remained in Monmouth after the family absconded to Texas and was one of the main sources of income that Mary had been relying on throughout the years. He was a journeyman joiner when the family left, and he now owned his own company. Richard had always been good with his hands, and while that had always been turned to mischief up until now, Howard allowed him to make use of all the boundless nervous energy that seemed to flood his littlest brother. Such an outright display of nepotism as hiring him into his own company wouldn't have gone down well among his workers, but there were plenty of joiners in Monmouth, and they all helped each other out where they could. In this case, that meant finding a job for an untrained and untested hand in a work crew that was already stretched near its limit.

Richard didn't make the full wage of a craftsman when he first started out, but he wasn't doing a full craftsman job. His role, from dawn until dusk, was to sand boards of plaster flat. It was mindless, repetitive, deathly boring work that nonetheless could cost you a finger if you got lazy and distracted while you were doing it — the worst kind of work that any apprentice joiner might ever have had to face. Richard took to it like a fish to water. His broken mind, usually incapable of holding onto a rational thought for more than a few hours at a time, seemed to be ideal for this kind of work. He locked onto the task and could perform it perfectly after he'd been shown how. His new boss wondered if he had been handed some sort of natural-born joiner and considered moving him on to other training immediately. But the truth of the matter was, those sheets still needed sanding down, and there was nobody about that could do them better or faster than Richard. If nothing else, he was able to sing Richard's praises to Howard, and in turn, Howard was reassured that his wastrel of a younger brother wasn't going to bring shame to him. He'd staked a small part of his reputation as a business owner on Richard's ability to do the job he'd been given, and Richard had provided no comfort in that regard since his arrival.

While he'd saved a little nest egg of cash from his burglary back in Dallas, Richard had spent the first few months in

Monmouth living off his brother's kindness and drinking his wages. Howard wasn't like Gene back in Chicago; he didn't try to bully Richard and make him do as he was told. He believed that his brother was a grown man, free to make a grown man's mistakes, but it did fill him with dread each time Richard came staggering home in the early hours of the morning.

With their lifestyles being so obviously in conflict, Howard was relieved when Richard announced that he was going to be moving out, even if it was only to the Christy Hotel in the middle of town. Richard claimed that the hotel was just a stepping stone until he'd saved enough to rent somewhere, but the truth was pretty obvious — he wanted to be closer to the taverns that he loved so dearly.

He settled into his new hotel room on the twenty-fifth of March, paying two weeks in advance without flinching. Richard intended on staying right where he was until further notice. The hotel was the cheapest he could find, but it was still more expensive than living for free on his brother's couch. To make his finances even tighter, he'd made some friends in Monmouth who were inciting him to drain his savings — a few men who could vaguely remember him from his school days, but mostly co-workers in the building trade, who had little respect for the work that he did but a lot of respect for the way that the man could drink.

Richard had never faced encouragement to drink before, and he revelled in the attention that his drunken antics bought him from his new friends. As a group, they decided to take a drinking tour of Gulf Point, Illinois, on the last weekend of the month. The rest of the group came back on Monday in time for work. Richard did not.

In the bathroom of one of the bars where they'd been drinking, some local had made a joke about Richard, trying to join in with the fun and games that the group had been carrying out in the tavern all night. Richard didn't see the funny side of the man's comments. He dragged him away from the urinal, slammed him against the grimy tiles and held a knife to his throat. Some of Richard's friends heard the commotion and rushed in to drag the two men apart, but the local man wasn't content to let things lie. He reported Richard to the police at the first chance he got, and the bar crawl ended for him in a night behind bars.

He made it back into Monmouth late on Monday afternoon and went straight to work to make his apologies. They'd already heard all about his stupidity. He didn't lose his job, but he was given a final warning; one more missed day and he'd be out.

Richard was in a very tenuous position. On the one hand, he had the threat of unemployment hanging over him each day that he went to work, but on the other, he was finally being set to tasks that were more interesting than sanding plasterboards. The local tavern, Frank's Place, had requested a pigpen be constructed around the backside of their building to save the titular owner from having to haul slops and waste back to his nearby farmhouse to feed his swine. Richard was given the whole job to handle himself. The work that he did may not have been the prettiest, but it was certainly solid, and his employer was impressed that a young man with practically no training could knock something like that together so easily.

Professionally, he seemed to be an asset, but personally, Richard had begun making abusive comments to his co-workers under the guise of humour, obviously trying to pick a fight while maintaining some sort of plausible deniability under his guise as a barroom clown. It was never enough to start a fight, although it often came close, and it was never enough to lay the man off, but it was a constant source of friction, and that was conveyed to Richard pretty clearly. He was aware that one day his needling would go too far and his job would disappear. So, he needed more money, and fast, if he wanted to maintain the lifestyle he was so enjoying.

Cash was one of his concerns, but romance was another. He hadn't had sex since January when Shirley had filed officially for divorce and sent him off into the spiral of rage that had cost him his comfy domestic role above Ginny's Lounge. The presence of his now-revered sister, Martha, had been enough to curb his animal instincts for a time, but now that he had his own place, far from anyone who might report his perversions back to her, there was nothing holding him back. In theory, he could've dated, but his experiences with the opposite sex to date had soured him to the idea. More importantly, no woman would have anything to do with him as his less-than-enlightened view of women was blurted out all too frequently and loudly in his conversations with his friends.

Once again, Richard was at a precipice. He could turn away from his course in the way that many misogynists do, masking his true feelings and acting like a decent man so that women would give him the time of day. Alternatively, he could dive right off that edge into an even deeper darkness of cruelty, loathing and depravity. He hung there for days, in limbo between the two available courses. Then, on the second of April, a message arrived from his mother. Shirley had been granted the divorce in his absence.

Already teetering on the edge, Richard dove directly into the deep end. This was the final insult in a long torrent of them, and he would take no more. Women. Whores. They were the bane of his existence, and until he asserted some control over them, he would know no peace. He went on the kind of drinking binge that would turn lesser men's livers to pâté, and in his inebriated state, all of the inhibitions and fears that usually held him back fell away, just as they had that fateful night he'd charged at a woman with a knife.

Mrs Virgil Harris was a divorcee in her late sixties and lived in one of the newly built houses that the teenaged Richard Speck had liked to sleep off his binges in. She was in the heart of his old familiar territory, lived alone, and knew absolutely nothing about Richard — the perfect combination of attributes for a victim. On the evening of the second of April, while Richard was drinking away his morality, she was working as a babysitter to make ends meet. The divorce late in her life had left little in the way of savings, and while she owned her house, which had all been paid for before the separation, she was living on scraps from day to day. On the night in question, she'd worked through until one o'clock in the morning on the third of April, sitting in the house of one of her neighbours, listening to the radio and checking up on their sleeping baby every hour or so. She wouldn't take any more money than the two and a half dollars that they'd agreed to begin with, even though they'd been out for hours longer than planned. She needed the money, but she wouldn't take it out of the pocket of a young couple just trying to get their start in life. Her morals meant more to her than a full stomach.

From the moment that she stepped through her door, she knew that something was wrong. For the sake of keeping her fuel costs down, she always had her windows closed and all the warmth of the day trapped inside come nightfall. But tonight, there was a chill as she entered the kitchen through her back door. She paused in the doorway, but already she could see a man stepping out of the shadows, moonlight glinting off the blade of his knife. 'Close the door behind you, please ma'am'.

Throughout the rest of the night, the tall white man with a soft southern drawl remained impeccably polite to Mrs Harris. He was polite as he tied her up and blindfolded her. Polite as he ransacked her house. Polite as he raked through her purse for the two dollars and fifty cents she'd earned that night, and even more impeccably polite as he carefully placed her on the kitchen table, stripped off her undergarments and raped her. He even said thank you and goodnight after he was done.

She was more bewildered by the experience than frightened, and in the end, her robber made off with only her radio, some pieces of costume jewellery that were worth practically nothing and the money that she'd made for babysitting. She gave a vague description to the police of her attacker, but there wasn't enough to even bring Richard in for questioning.

This evil and pointless act still wasn't enough to abate Richard's rage. He'd been confused by the age of Mrs Harris. He hadn't been able to see her as the whore he wanted to punish so much as the mother he wanted to love him. It'd tempered his actions in a way that displeased him. He hated that he didn't have control of himself, even when he was trying so hard to exert his control over the world around him. The rape had been insufficient to satisfy him — it lacked violence; it lacked domination. He needed more.

Less than a week later, the very same rage against women reared up in him unexpectedly when he didn't have the time to plan out a safe outlet for it. He was out drinking in Frank's Place when a bartender cracked a friendly joke at his expense. He stormed out of the place, unnoticed by the crowd that were too busy enjoying themselves to worry about his predilection for sulking off. He already had a lot of baggage relating to female bartenders not giving him enough respect, and the fact that the bitch was stomping around with his saint of a mother's name and calling him names was too much to handle. Just a month before, he had been doing good work as a joiner and getting paid for it at this very bar, and even the place he once found so comforting stung now that unemployment loomed over him with crushing inevitability if he ever sidled back to work. It was too much to stand; the straw that broke the camel's back.

He stomped out to look at the pigpen, now fully populated with swine, and remind himself that he'd built it, that he was capable of things that nobody could have guessed at. He was more than just a criminal. More than just a nobody. It didn't matter how the whores and the barflies tried to tear him down; he'd made this place with his own two hands. He didn't need their approval. He didn't need any of them. Even his brother had cut ties with him in the wake of his arrest in Gulf Point, no longer asking after him through common friends in the trade and doing his best to distance himself from the wild young man he had the misfortune of being bound to by blood. Richard didn't need any of them, and he certainly didn't need the whores to love him.

All of these thoughts were tumbling through his head, end over end, as he stared down into the writhing mass of muddy pigs. He was so lost in thought that he didn't even hear footsteps behind him until it was too late. 'Richard? What are you doing out here, honey? I'm sorry. Did I hurt your feelings back there?'

The bartender. Mary Kay Pierce. It was like the stars had aligned. Mary Kay was the sister-in-law of the owner of the titular Frank of Frank's place, a professional with years of experience working in the service industry. She'd been wrangling drunks since she was a teenager, from the sobbing romantics to the vicious screamers. One sulking manual labourer giving her the cold shoulder and staring at the pigs really shouldn't have been beyond the limits of her talents. She slipped an arm around Richard's shoulders. 'I'm sorry, buddy. You're one of the good ones. I shouldn't have jibed you'.

Richard's face was blank as he turned. His vacant eyes took her in like she wasn't even human, like she was just an object to be manipulated. He had experience in bars, too, on the other side of the equation. He knew when he was being condescended to, when some whore thought that she could handle him. He'd also had plenty of experience in bar brawls. He wasn't one of the drunken idiots who just flung his arms around, not anymore. When you're the smallest man in the bar, you learn how to fight right from an early age.

His fist rose from his hip as he turned, twisting as it hammered into her gut. He hit her so hard that it lifted her clean off her feet, and when he let her drop, she found that all the strength had fled her body and her legs couldn't support her anymore. Mary collapsed in a heap, gasping for air and finding none. She could taste copper in her mouth.

He didn't just know how to hit, Richard knew how to wound. With that single punch, he'd ruptured Mary's liver. He'd killed her with a single blow; she just didn't know it yet. She tried to scream, but there wasn't enough air left in her lungs to make anything more than a whimper as he took a firm grip on the roots of her hair and dragged her forward. With a little grunt of effort, he lifted her up and then tipped her over the fence, eyes darting back towards the bar, where he could hear the patrons pouring out into the pitch-black night after the last call for orders was over. They were unbelievably close to the street lights and detection. Just one head turned the wrong way could cost Richard everything. Clambering into the pen after her, kicking the pigs out of his way, Richard dragged Mary further into the pigsty and further from any hope of help or salvation. The pigs squealed as he pulled her through the mud, but their noise just served to mask the feeble whimpers that Mary was finally managing to work past her lips. In the deep shadows of the little shelter that he'd built to keep the pigs out of the rain, he finally laid her down and started pulling at her mud-sodden clothes. Blood was pooling on her lips now, working its way up her throat now that she was laid flat. But even so, she fought him, her feeble arms batting at him as he tried to strip her bare. She already knew that something inside of her was broken, but she wouldn't give him the pleasure of her body while she still had life within her. With hooked fingers, she scratched at his face, but he jerked back out of reach, treading on one of the curious pigs and setting it squealing all over again. Distantly, he could hear voices. Paranoia took hold. The pigs must have attracted attention. Someone could be coming from the bar to find out what all the racket was. He bolted.

Alone in the mud and the dark, Mary finally let her arms fall limp to her sides and drew in her last bloody breath.

The murder was the talk of Monmouth by late morning. Everyone had known Mary. She was well-liked about town, and her death shook the small community to its core. The police sprang into action in an uncharacteristic flurry of activity. They parsed as many accounts of the night as possible, placed Richard in the bar and made the connection between him and the pigpen where Mary's brother-in-law had found her. They had no real suspicion that Richard was responsible for the crime, but nonetheless, they had to question him — something that was easier said than done when the man had no fixed address in town. Eventually, they settled on contacting his boss and asking for a call if he ever showed up to work. In turn, his boss baited the hook with the promise of Richard's last paycheque if he would show up to collect it.

The next day, Richard got his money, but he walked out into the waiting arms of the police. He proved to be more evasive than they were accustomed to. The boy who'd faltered in the face of authority had been burned away by a real jail term. He had no more respect for the police than he did anyone else at this point. He admitted that he was at the bar but claimed he'd left earlier in the evening. He admitted that he'd built the pigpens, but that had been more than a month ago. He didn't have any particular attachment to Frank's Place or any of the staff there. He had no quarrel with anyone there, either. It was just one of the few bars about town that he happened to frequent.

At the end of the impromptu interview in the back of a squad car, they insisted on dropping Richard home at his hotel. They took note of his room number and asked him politely to stay in town for a few days in case they had follow-up questions. He laughed. 'Where else am I going to go?'

As the days went on and the investigation proceeded, it became clear that the timeline that Richard had presented to the police was not entirely accurate. There still wasn't enough there to make him suspicious in the eyes of the police — heavy drinking tends to distort the memory somewhat — but it was enough that they felt the need to take another pass at him.

On the eighteenth, that was exactly what they did, arriving at the Christy Hotel and heading up to his room. It was abandoned. They nabbed the desk clerk and demanded answers, but he had nothing useful to say. Richard had come down with a suitcase full of clothes, announced he was taking them to the laundromat and then vanished earlier on in the day, but none of that was particularly unusual. He was happy to let the police into Richard's room to wait for him, and it was there that it became even clearer that he'd fled town. Just a cursory inspection of his room revealed the stolen jewellery and radio from the house of Mrs Harris and an abundance of other goods that had gone missing in various burglaries around Monmouth in the past few months. There was no physical evidence tying him to the murder of Mary, but the fact that he'd fled town when the police made contact with him was enough to raise some eyebrows all on its own.

Richard had begun to learn his lessons about law enforcement. He didn't run the moment that the police were out of sight. He took some time to do his own investigation and confirm that he wasn't being watched before he left, even taking the time to pack his belongings and leave behind anything that might incriminate him during his flight. He would never be a criminal genius — his impulsive nature and limited attention span had seen to that — but he was capable of learning.

The police searched for him thoroughly around Monmouth, but he'd jumped on a freight train as it passed through, keeping his name off any official paper trail that might lead the police after him. The train's destination was, somewhat inevitably, Chicago.

The Angel in White

On his return to Chicago, he knew that he was going to have to fabricate some sort of story to placate Martha and make himself into a victim of circumstance rather than a criminal on the run. He truly believed that his sister would take him in without question, but that husband of hers was another matter. Gene had watched Richard lingering around their house the last time with a steely glare fixed on the younger man from dawn until dusk. If there was any sign that Richard was involved in any wrongdoing, he'd have his brother-in-law out on the streets faster than he could blink.

The tale that he spouted after showing up unannounced on their doorstep was like something out of the kind of adventure serials that you might find in a comic book — that a syndicate of criminals in the little town of Monmouth had targeted Richard and insisted that he sell drugs on their behalf. He'd refused, because he was so morally upstanding, but had to flee town after threats were made on his life. It was ridiculous but so ridiculous that it was hard to dispute. If Richard had provided a lie that even vaguely touched on real life, then Martha might've known how to pick it apart, but something this bizarre was beyond her. In the dark of the night, she found herself whispering to Gene, 'It's so crazy that it has to be true. Nobody in their right mind could make a story like that up'.

Gene worked nights as a railroad switchman, and he was uncomfortable at the prospect of leaving Richard alone at night with his teenage girls. Never enough to outright say anything about it to his wife, but enough that it preyed on his imagination while he was trying to do his job. Very quickly, he settled on the idea that he needed to find Richard a job to get him out of the house, preferably a job somewhere well away from his family.

After the sweet release of murdering Mary Kay Pierce, Richard's rage had fallen silent for the first time in his life. He felt like he was in control of his actions, like he could finally be calm for the first time since his father died and his mother brought that peg-legged salesman home. Raping her first would've been better, there was no doubt about that, but killing was a whole other kind of pleasure, something that he'd never experienced before in his life. Violence and sex had coexisted in his life before now, but they'd never been intrinsically linked. Rape had always been more pleasurable than sex because it didn't come with the internal conflict that a consenting partner inflicted on him, and because it gave him a feeling of power over the women who controlled everything in the world in his eyes. But deriving pleasure from hurting a woman was something entirely new to him, a whole new world of potential delights that he'd just stepped into for the very first time.

In the meantime, he planned to cultivate a relationship with Martha untainted by his darker impulses. She'd be the perfect pure mother figure for him if he could just get around her husband.

Five days passed, with Richard hanging around the house, drinking only enough to curb his headaches but still making everyone just a little uncomfortable. His attempts to cosy up to Martha were going nowhere. She didn't understand why he was so intent on winning her over, and the cloying attempts to ingratiate himself fell flat more often than not. Unlike his real mother, Martha had no obligation to love Richard, and having him in her home all the time was already pushing the limits of family loyalty for her without his constant strange attempts to get her to take care of him.

Attempts at conversation with Gene drew that same blank stare Richard was coming to suspect was aggression. The only ones who were close to his age and willing to talk were his nieces, and Gene monitored every moment that he was with them like a hawk, ensuring they were stowed away in their room before heading out to work in the evening.

Loneliness began to dog Richard again. The relationship that he imagined having with his sister would not come to fruition, the bar scene was denied to him due to his lack of money and he was in withdrawal from a half-dozen illicit substances that he could no longer source. He was reaching a crisis point yet again, the internal pressures that drove him to violence building up past the point of tolerance, just waiting for an outlet.

Gene had been silently observing Richard through all of this, watching his frustration growing. He needed to get the man out of the house, now. On his sixth day in the house, Richard was woken from his shallow sleep on the family sofa by a sharp prod. Gene, freshly returned from his night shift, was talking directly to him for the first time. 'Get up. I'm taking you out to get work'.

Richard had all of his usual excuses ready, but Gene cut them all off. 'There's steady work on the ships if you're strong enough to handle the work. Have you got what it takes?'

Before his settled family life, Gene had been in the U.S. Navy, and many of his old friends had migrated into a civilian life at sea in the Merchant Navy. It paid well, and it gave men like Richard someplace to be, well away from any of the dangers or temptations of land-bound life. It was the perfect solution to Gene's mind, and he'd been making quiet enquiries with his friends about how to proceed.

Unable to turn down the implicit challenge to his manhood, Richard was up, dressed and loaded in the car within a few minutes. Gene couldn't believe how easy it'd been. Before anyone was allowed to sail, they needed a letter of authority signed off by the Coast Guard. At their offices, Richard was fingerprinted, given a physical examination and photographed for his apprentice seaman's license. The next day, he was able to pick up his documentation and start looking for a berth at the National Maritime Union hiring hall, an unassuming building in the Jeffery Manor neighbourhood of Chicago, just one block east of a row of six brick townhouses that would later become the focal point of a whole nation's horror.

With his letter of authority in hand and a clean bill of health, Richard was a head above most of the other men looking for work. He found a berth immediately on the Clarence B. Randall, a bulk ore lake freighter that had stopped in Chicago on its way upriver.

The Randall departed on the thirtieth of April, and Richard was able to carry all of his worldly possessions on board in a single sack. He pressed a kiss to his sister's cheek, endured a crushing handshake from Gene and then was off up the ramp to the waiting crew of hard-eyed men just waiting for him to make a mistake so that they could justify replacing him at the next port. It wasn't welcoming, but it wasn't the worst situation Richard had gone strolling into, not by a long shot.

Life on the boat was hard on Richard at first. He wasn't accustomed to having his every move dictated to him. Even in prison, he'd always experienced a degree of autonomy compared to life onboard a ship. It was the kind of discipline that his life had always lacked, and surrounded by other men, far from the temptations that had always plagued him, Richard suddenly found himself sober, attentive and respected. The background static in his mind had finally faded to more tolerable levels. The headaches that had defined his chaotic life no longer haunted his every waking hour, only afflicting him when he dreamed. It was the kind of life that might have made him, if not normal, then at least acceptable to a functioning society. Knowing what he should be doing at any given moment, knowing that he was serving a purpose higher than the base pursuit of his next grunting moment of pleasure, it suited him well. For the first time, he began to be moulded by his surroundings into something more than he had been. He started to grow as a person, to learn, to become incrementally better.

On the third of May, just a few days after departure, fate intervened. It was as though the universe couldn't tolerate a version of Richard, who was anything more than a monster. He didn't show up to his scheduled shift, so the captain sent one of the other men down to rouse him. They found Richard curled in the foetal position on the floor in his cabin, so hot to the touch that it was startling. There wasn't a doctor on board, but there was enough medical experience between the men that it was obvious their new recruit was riddled with some sort of infection and burning up with fever. Richard was barely lucid, doubled over with the pain and struggling to speak. His appendix had swollen to the size of a grapefruit, and it was ready to burst. With no small amount of grumbling, the ship came to a halt and a helicopter was called out to retrieve the sickly seaman. He was airlifted to the Keweenaw Peninsula in Michigan, to St Joseph's Hospital in Hancock, where he was rushed into surgery for an emergency appendectomy. When he woke in the hospital, he was quite sure that he'd died and gone to heaven.

The drugs at the hospital wiped away all of the pain he'd been enduring since coming off his own cocktail of illicit medications, and after just a short while at sea away from his obsession with women, he now found them all around him. Beautiful, young women in hospital white, like angels flocking every time he turned his head. Pure women who didn't look at him with contempt or cruelty, who weren't out to get everything that they could from him before they moved on to the next sucker. They treated him with such kindness; it was all that he could do to keep from weeping. When he awoke from his surgery, doped to the eyeballs on morphine, he opened his eyes to find the prettiest girl he'd ever seen sitting by his bedside, holding his hand.

Judy Laakaniemi was a 28-year-old nurse's aide who'd found her life outside of the hospital abruptly cut short when her husband filed for divorce. Despite these struggles, she still had more than enough kindness to spare for all of her patients, and she soon discovered the deep well of loneliness at the core of Richard that was hurting him considerably more than his slow-healing stitches. She would sit with him daily, talking to him about his life and about her own.

For the first time, Richard was confronted with a woman treating him like a human being, like a friend. It was an excruciating experience for a man with such a concrete worldview on the nature of gender. She was no whore, but neither could she be called pure. He had heard enough of her history to know that she'd lain with a man before, her husband — and others — yet he felt no revulsion towards her. He felt no compulsion to punish her for her promiscuity.

Confusion was always at the root of Richard's violent acts. Each time that he'd committed one of his atrocities up until this point, it was because his worldview had been challenged, and ultimately the undemanding kindness of Judy was the greatest challenge he'd ever faced. She was good to him for no reason, to no benefit for herself. He couldn't understand it. He spent long nights staring up at the flickering fluorescents and trying to puzzle through it, trying to work out what angle she was trying to play and how she was planning to screw him over. He couldn't work it out. Even when his last day in the hospital came, and she swept him into a hug, he still couldn't work out what she was after, and he left the hospital in his sister's care with that seed of confusion taking root.

Life at Gene and Martha's house was not greatly improved from his last stay, and as the opioids that he'd been sent away with began to fade, Richard soon descended into a fresh hell. Now that he'd experienced real friendship with Judy, he could see how shallow his relationship with his sister had become. The fact that both women had been nurses in their life only amplified what Richard had already suspected — Martha wasn't the kindly mother figure that he'd been seeking all this time. She was cold to him, deliberately creating distance between them whenever he tried to have a personal conversation with her. From the outside, it may be obvious why she was so reluctant to get closer to the black sheep of her family, but to Richard, it just seemed like the same slight played out over and over again. The rejection stung at him as much as his wound. It felt just as sickly as when his mother had rejected him in favour of Carl Lindberg.

Gene was no Carl, but his disapproval of Richard was just as palpable, and it drove him out of the man's sight as soon as was humanly possible. On 20 May, just a week after his release from hospital, Richard was back on the Clarence B. Randall, trying to get back into the flow of things. His wound had barely scarred over, and he was already throwing his weight around to prove that he was the match of the more experienced men. It hurt him constantly, and withdrawal from his painkillers was setting off headaches frequently, but still, he persevered, trying to prove himself the match of these men and step out of the ever-present shadow that he felt Gene was casting over him. He began to drink to help with his various pains, but that made him increasingly sloppy as he went about his work. The officers had been waiting to find out exactly what was wrong with Richard, and alcoholism seemed like a likely explanation for why the man might go to sea. They didn't come down hard on him, but they didn't lighten his workload, either. They made it clear through their actions that if he could handle his liquor, they would look the other way, but if he couldn't, he'd be punished like any other sailor.

This state of affairs continued until 14 June, when Richard confronted one of the Randall's officers while in a drunken rage. He was put ashore immediately, sacked without pay or recourse and left to make his own way back to Chicago. Once he arrived in Chicago, he couldn't face the disapproving glares of Martha and

Gene. He found a bed for himself in St Elmo's, an East Chicago flophouse on 99th Street and South Ewing Avenue, to keep himself under their radar. Running low on funds, and with no other recourse but to slink home with his tail between his legs, Richard bought himself a train ticket to Houghton, Michigan.

Judy met him at the train station with a smile — the first friendly face he'd seen in weeks. She took him to get settled at Douglas House, a local hostel, then out for lunch. The two of them caught up within minutes, with Richard too ashamed to share too much about the circumstances of his sudden unemployment and Judy too uncomfortable to delve into the details of her messy divorce, which seemed to be dominating all of her time outside of work. Even with those parts of themselves held back, the duo had no trouble filling up the hours of the afternoon, and when it came time to part ways, Judy pulled Richard into another hug that left him even more confused than before, his confusion exacerbated even further when she slipped an envelope into his hand and wished him a safe journey home and good luck with the job hunt. The envelope contained $80 from her savings that she'd taken out to help him through his time of hardship.

He slept poorly in the hostel's narrow cot, troubling thoughts setting the static of his usual internal conflicts aflame. She was a woman. There was no denying that fact, but she didn't fit into either of the categories that women could be assigned. Judy made no sense. Come morning, he made the trip back to Chicago with more money in his pocket than he'd had in ages but no compulsion to spend it on liquor either. He had the vague impression that he'd be letting his angel Judy down if he were to do a thing like drink her charity away, and the fact that he succumbed to that imagined disapproval rather than doing as he pleased just served to agitate him more. He was being controlled, and he didn't even understand how.

Twenty-Five Dollars of Fun

Gene and Martha opened their doors to Richard one last time on his return to Chicago, but their disapproval was apparent. They wanted him gone as soon as possible, and it became Gene's routine to drive Richard down to the NMU hiring hall each morning before he turned in for another day's fitful rest. News spread fast around the union, and nobody wanted a drunkard who fought with officers on their crew.

Day after day, he was returned to the hall, and day after day he was rejected by everyone. On the 8th July, he was granted a berth on the SS Flying Spray, a cargo ship bound for South Vietnam, only to discover when he arrived at the ship that his place had been sniped by a seaman with more seniority in the union who'd received a phone call about the berth from his friends. Richard was apoplectic with rage, and he spent the whole weekend complaining, ranting and raving about the unfairness of the situation until finally Gene and Martha were out of patience.

Come Monday, they drove him into town with his one suitcase and dumped him by the side of the road. He was old enough to take care of himself, and Martha was tired of trying to keep him happy. She had her own life to attend to, and it was falling apart with Richard's constant interruptions to their routine. Gene smiled at Richard for the first time when he told the man he was no longer welcome in their home. It was only for a moment, but it was enough to confirm all of Richard's suspicions that the other man had been out to get him from the beginning.

Richard lugged his bag a mile to the Vets' Park neighbourhood of South Deering, Chicago, and picked out the least depressing rooming house he could find, a place called 'Pauline's'. Once he had his bag in a room and a key in his hand, he set out to find himself a drink. Judy might not have approved, but at least she would have understood. He'd been rejected again, this time by the sister who should've treated him the kindest, the woman he was convinced was going to be his new, better mother. Martha, who'd been a nurse, just like his angel, who should've been brimming over with kindness and compassion. He couldn't stand it. She'd chosen that worm Gene over her own flesh and blood, just because the man didn't like a little competition in the household for top dog. It was pathetic. Richard drank all of his savings, all of Judy's savings really, as those same thoughts whipped back and forth through his mind. And then, when the grimy tavern finally turned him out onto the street, he staggered back to Pauline's. Round and round spun the dingy little room, and round and round went Richard's train of thought, stuck in a terminal spiral towards destruction, drawing closer and closer to the black void at the core of his mind with every turn.

When the morning of 12 July, came, Richard awoke with a head full of pain and thoughts that felt like broken glass if he pondered them for too long. He rose from his bed, dressed as well as he could, packed up his bag and made the long trudge across town to the hiring hall. He lingered around, reeking of liquor and groaning at every sound louder than a whisper until mid-afternoon when, finally, a berth came up for him. The SS Sinclair Great Lakes was an oil tanker docked in East Chicago,

Indiana — the kind of local, long-standing berth that most seamen in town would've killed for. Unfortunately for them, by lunchtime, the majority of them had sauntered off home, leaving only the truly desperate, or those with nowhere else to go, behind. Hating himself for it, but with no other choice, Richard called up Gene and asked him for a ride. His new job was a half-hour away by car, and he had no money to get a taxi.

Gene came and got him and drove him across to Indiana with a smug little grin on his face. After all of Richard's posturing and strut, he'd still come crawling back like a little lost boy the minute that his drinking money ran out. Gene didn't see it as a sign of maturity that Richard was asking for help when he needed it, any more than Richard saw this whole exercise as anything less than completely humiliating. They arrived at the docks, and Gene stepped out of the car for a smoke while he waited for Richard's papers to be approved. It took less than a minute before Richard came roaring back down the ramp onto the docks, cursing at the top of his lungs and spitting all over the place. Yet again, he'd missed out on his berth, although this time, it seemed to have been due to a miscommunication rather than someone sniping it.

All the way back to Chicago, Gene lectured him on responsibility, warning him that he couldn't just drop everything each time his little brother-in-law needed a ride. Richard turned beet red early in the trip, and the flush didn't leave him until he was dumped back at the roadside. There wasn't a chance in hell that he was going to put himself through that shameful experience again. He'd rather miss out on a berth than have to deal with that sanctimonious prick driving him there.

Richard had nothing left, not a penny to his name or a place to hang his hat, so he hiked out of town once more, eyes turned to the houses around him, searching for the tell-tale signs of construction in progress. With a likely place in sight, he located a local Shell petrol station that would let him stow his bag behind the counter; then, he tucked himself in among the debris of a partially demolished house to sleep fitfully through the night. Tomorrow would be a better day. It had to be.

The next morning, Wednesday the 13th of July, Richard found himself covered in early morning dew when he creaked awake. A night sleeping rough might've been fine for a teenager, but to a man coming down from years of drug abuse and recovering from surgery, it was a profoundly bad and painful idea. He ached as he made his way to the Shell garage to collect his things, and his legs felt heavy as he made his way back across town to the Union Hall. The hall didn't open until nine, so he was left lurking on its doorstep for almost an hour before a car pulled up alongside him and tooted its horn. Martha was inside. Gene drove around the corner to park beside an elementary school, and Richard climbed in the back, leaving his case propped up against the side of the car.

None of them mentioned his banishment from the family home. None of them picked at the old wounds that they'd all rather were left alone. For half an hour, they shared each other's company, with Martha hoping that a little time together before Richard shipped out might ease her conscience, with Gene gloating ever so slightly to himself that he'd rid himself of the loathsome pest. At the end of the talk, and to Gene's dismay, Martha compounded her attempts to mend bridges by giving Richard all the money that she had in her purse so that he would at least have a roof over his head for one more night. It was obvious that he'd been sleeping outside from his aroma alone. All that she had came to a grand total of $25. Richard took it because he was in no position to do otherwise, but his mind still turned back to Judy and the much greater kindness she'd bestowed on him with no need for guilt to spurn her on. Judy had tried to help because she was a good person. Martha was trying to help because she felt bad. For the first time, the dichotomy between the two women became completely clear to Richard. Like their mother before her, Martha was just another whore.

Back on the street, Richard made his way along to the NMU hall to look for work, but after just half an hour of hanging around, he thought better of it. There'd be no work for him; he knew that now. Every man in that hall had seniority over him, and even if they didn't, after all of the screw-ups on his first trip out, he knew that nobody was going to take him on. The whole exercise was pointless. He was wasting their time, and he was wasting his own time. He stood up abruptly and headed for the door. By half-past ten in the morning, the town was starting to warm up and liven up. The ache that had nestled itself in his bones through the night was burnt away by the warmth of the sun, and the girls were strolling by in their summer dresses. Things were looking up already. A man could have a lot of fun in Chicago with just $25.

His first stop was across town on East 100th Street, home of the Shipyard Inn, a run-down flophouse that sailors sometimes frequented when they were down on their luck or pinching their pennies. It was the cheapest rooming house in town, and while he didn't have any plans to sleep just yet, having a space of his own brought a little calm back into Richard. This place was his, even if the rest of the world had fallen into chaos. This one room was under his control. Even now, as his whole life spiralled out of control, he could control this.

With those few dollars accounted for, the rest had him set up to have a much more enjoyable day, and who knew what fresh fortune might find its way to him. Richard had long ago accepted that the world was in a constant state of flux, but he wasn't so nihilistic as to believe that he could never end up on top in the midst of it. Sometimes the flotsam and jetsam of life contained treasures.

There was no shortage of taverns and bars around the Shipyard Inn. You could almost say that was the entirety of the appeal of the place, and Richard spent the morning taking a tour and seeing the local sights. He would have a few drinks in one bar before bouncing to the next, never lingering long enough to stick in anyone's memory. He'd learned his lesson from Monmouth — if he wanted to get in trouble and get away from the consequences, then he couldn't linger in one place for too long.

As the morning faded in a drunken haze into the afternoon, the $25 began to dwindle, and the faces started to get familiar. Richard wasn't the only one doing the tour around the local bars. There were working girls doing the rounds, confident that Richard was going to pick one of them to head home with before the end of the day. They weren't strictly incorrect.

Richard's drink of choice was Jim Beam and Coke, and by the third rotation through the bars, they were being served up to him without his even needing to ask. They weren't cheap, however, and by mid-afternoon, Richard was flat broke. He was nursing his last drink, leaning heavily on the jukebox for stability, when Ella Mae Hooper approached him. She was 53 years old but caked in makeup. In the dim light of a bar, she was a handsome enough woman to turn his head. She pressed up against him to whisper in his ear, well-versed in the delicate art of persuading potential clients. The two of them left the bar hand in hand, both with only one thing on their mind — parting the other from their money.

Back in his room at the Shipyard Inn, Richard drew his knife on Ella Mae and demanded she hand over her money. In turn, Ella Mae pulled her .22-calibre Rohm revolver out of her purse and levelled it at his head. It wasn't a big and impressive gun — it was a Saturday night special that she'd got on mail order — but it had always been enough to protect her from clients with cruel intentions. Tonight, it did her no good. Richard snatched the gun from her hand, pressed the knife to her neck and rode her down onto the bed. 'I was hoping you'd fight back'.

The rape was brief but brutal. With the knife, there was no real need for violence, but he still slapped her in the face over and over, just like he had with his wife when she refused him what he felt was his due. When he was finished, he took the little money that Ella Mae had in her purse and tossed her out onto the streets, keeping the gun for himself.

There wasn't enough money from that robbery to last him more than a day or so, but that didn't much matter. He had plans to commit a burglary that night to refill his coffers, a score big enough to get him right out of Chicago if he wanted. He knew exactly the place that he was going to hit, somewhere full of soft, weak women who'd give him whatever he wanted the minute he barked at them. He'd been eyeing them up for weeks now, counting them going in and out of their townhouse while he smoked outside the NMU hiring hall.

Dressed all in black with a knife on his belt, another in his pocket and the pistol tucked into his waistband, Richard headed out for dinner at Kay's Pilot House a few blocks away. Ella Mae had already fled back home, bruised and bleeding.

After a hearty meal, the first he'd had in days, Richard returned to the Shipyard Inn and settled himself in the bar beneath the rooms. If it was possible, this bar was even more low-rent than the others that he'd been frequenting throughout the day, with open drug use in addition to heavy drinking of rotgut whiskey. With cash in his pocket and more coming, Richard decided to splash out on himself. He'd always enjoyed pills, so why not try the next step up. It didn't cost him much to acquire some heroin and a syringe, and the addicts were more than happy to talk him through the best way to take his new medicine.

Peace rushed through him at the press of the plunger. Peace and bliss. For the first time in his life, nothing hurt, and nothing was confusing. All of the barbed wire tangled in his skull felt like it was loosening, and he could finally see things clearly. He hung around the bar for a few more drinks, savouring the flavour of the bourbon for what felt like the first time in his life. A little after 10 o'clock in the evening, as the buzz of his first shot of heroin was starting to fade and real-world concerns were starting to make themselves known, Richard left the bar and started his mile-and-a-half-long trek across town to the NMU hiring hall and the house that he'd been staking out. He had a spring in his step. He had a plan in mind. All of the randomness that'd shaped his life up until this moment was forgotten, and he felt certain that he would remain in control, no matter what situation presented itself when he finally arrived at 2319 East 100th Street.

It Just Wasn't Their Night

There was no need to be coy; no need to be shy. It didn't matter if they were staring right at him, because he was the one in control. He was the one with the power. Not the women. Not the whores. Him.

He stepped sharply up to the door and rapped on it with his knuckles four times. By the time that somebody answered, he already had the revolver out on show. For a moment, just a moment, he was blinded by the light behind the young woman who opened the door, and he blinked lazily to clear his vision. She wasn't a little Filipino student nurse at all. She was that bitch Shirley Ann. He didn't know why she was young and pretty again, didn't know why she wouldn't look him in the face, but there was no mistaking her. It was Shirley, the source of all his pain and suffering. The whore who'd ruined his life.

Another blink cleared his vision. Corazon Amurao looked nothing like his ex-wife. She was a head shorter, built completely differently, not to mention being of a completely different ethnicity. She wasn't looking at his face because her eyes were locked on the gun in his hand. He was in control. Not the screaming in his head. Him. He stepped forward and took hold of the young exchange student by the forearm, driving her back into the hallway. He smiled at her, and when his words came, they were spoken in the same soft southern drawl that his victims had always reported. A voice so calm and collected compared to the tone he used screeching his business in everyday life that it was practically impossible to recognise. His real voice. The one that he'd always heard inside his head when his thoughts were untangled. 'Where are your companions?'

The corridor was lined with doors, and behind any one might've been another little delight just demanding his attention. A whorehouse, brimming over with them, all dressed up in their pretty nurses' uniforms like that could make them pure — like anyone would believe that these whores could be anything more than the filth they were. Another one of them burst out into the hallway, not in her nurses' uniform but in a nightgown. It didn't matter, Richard recognised her anyway. He pointed the pistol at Merlita's face, and all her colour drained away. With a wave of the gun, he herded them down the hall towards the bedroom at the end. He could hear snoring inside despite all the noise these two were making. Two were accounted for. There were eight of them in the house altogether. He'd counted them in and out often enough. He pushed Cora and Merlita right through the door at the end without pausing for breath. There were three asleep in here. Five total, three to go. Even as he thought that, another one stepped out of the bathroom at his side and gasped.

In every other part of his life, Richard felt like he was moving at half speed, like his brain wasn't firing at the same rate as everyone else's. It wasn't that he was stupid, just that there was so much else rattling around in his skull that sometimes it took a while for things to come out like he wanted them to. But not in a place like this or a time like this. He grabbed the new nurse by the hair and tossed her into the bedroom, knocking Merlita and Cora off their feet by brute force. Six of them. Two to go.

He turned to look back along the corridor, head cocked, but he couldn't hear the sound of any more motion in the house.

Strange. It was late for any of the girls to be out still. When he turned back to the bedroom, three of the girls had vanished out of sight, and for a moment, the steady thump of his heart stuttered. He couldn't have any of them running off and causing him trouble. That was when he noticed the movement of the closet door. They were hiding in there. Three grown women, cowering in the closet like he was the monster crawled out from under their bed. He rolled his eyes at the three women still in the room, grabbing the closest one, Pamela, around the waist as she clambered down from her top bunk and dragging her hard against the line of his body. 'It's all right. Calm it down. I ain't here to hurt nobody'.

Something about the offhand way he said it somehow cut through the panic. He wasn't much older than her, and he had such soft features and such a soft voice that it was hard to be afraid of him. 'Get them out here, would you?'

He let go of Pamela, and she walked over to the closet, casting fearful looks back at him all the way. The other two still hadn't moved from their bunk beds, so Richard kept the gun pointed in their direction. When they lurched into motion once the shock had worn off, he needed to be ready for them.

The other girls filed out of the cupboard, one by one. All in their nightgowns. All so very young and so very weak. Richard forced down the rush of arousal. Now was not the time. He had other things to attend to. Directing them at gun-point, Richard carefully arranged the girls in a semi-circle on the floor. 'Sit down. Take it easy. Sit down'.

Once they were all settled and he'd quieted the rebellious, baying part of his mind that wanted to rape, slaughter and revel in his power, Richard crouched down beside them and explained the situation. 'I ain't going to hurt anybody. I'm going to New Orleans. I just want some money'.

Nina and Pat were the ones he hadn't touched yet, so they were the bravest. 'Can we go and get our purses?'

'One at a time. And if I even think you're fooling around, I've got all your friends here waiting to pay for it'.

It was the first time he'd let anything even resembling a threat slip out, and he said it with such a casual tone that they barely even noticed until things were already in motion. One by one, the girls filed out of the room, fetched their purses, and then resumed their position in the circle. Richard took the cash with a rueful smile, like he was passing around the collection plate in church or accepting their charity on some street corner. The whole situation was made so much more surreal by how inoffensive their robber was. It was like they were all moving through some bad dream, never quite believing the evidence of their eyes. Richard was in a dream of his own. All of his fantasies about having women at his mercy were finally coming to fruition right before his eyes, and the heroin haze made it so easy to forget the lines that restraint and fear normally wouldn't let him cross. He turned to the girls with a big smile, wet his lips and opened his mouth to command them. That was when the front door of the townhouse burst open.

Gloria Davy was blind drunk when she staggered into the house. She'd been out on a date with her boyfriend and enjoyed herself thoroughly, as she always did. Now all that was left was to stagger to bed and try her best not to wake up the other girls. They were starting to get snippy with her for coming in late and wakening them up. When she saw the light was out under the bedroom door at the end of the corridor, she let out a groan. Everybody was sleeping. There would be complaints in the morning if she made a noise. It wasn't fair — just because they all lived like nuns, she had to have a bad time, too? She crept down the hall and eased the door open as silently as she could manage, but what she saw inside that bedroom dragged a guttural scream from her throat.

Richard lunged out and caught her, dragging her into the room and casting her down onto the floor in the same fluid movement. He was made for this. All the rest of his life, he moved through the world like a fish on land, but here, in a time like this, all of his instincts and motions flowed together perfectly. He became what he was meant to be in times of danger. He kicked the door behind him shut without a backwards glance and moved over to the nearest bed. He stripped off the sheet and drew a knife. The girls gasped at the sight of it, but none of them moved. This was how powerful whores really were. When they met a real man, capable of living a real-life, they cowered before him. This was the truth of whores. The only sound in the room was the tearing of cloth as he sliced the sheets into strips. Even the sobbing had stopped as they all watched him, doe-eyed, and waited to see what was going to happen next. 'I can't have you all running off and getting the police the minute I leave, so I'm just going to tie you up. Don't worry; I'll be gentle with you'.

Why did whores always believe him when he said he'd be gentle? If men were gentle, then whores would move on to the next sucker even faster. Yet it felt like they all wanted to hear the words even as their bodies demanded that Richard be anything but gentle. One by one, he took hold of the girls, drew a strip of ragged cloth out and bound their legs together. Next, he went around again and carefully bound their wrists together. Every girl was petrified, but even now, they believed his lies. They believed that he was just going to take the money and leave after they'd all seen his face.

Even when they were all tied up, he wouldn't leave. Even when he wouldn't leave, they still didn't say a word. They all just looked up at him with terror etched in every line of their faces, dimly illuminated by the yellow streetlamp glow from outside. Pamela was the last to be bound up. He'd kept her for last with good reason. He kept saying, 'I just want to talk to her. That's all. I just want to talk to her alone'.

Pamela whimpered as the friction of the carpet burned the back of her thighs, but she didn't cry out, and she didn't fight back. In the side bedroom where she'd spent so many months sleeping in peace alone, he loomed over her. Without any struggle or argument, she just lay there, waiting for him to do whatever he wanted to do. When did whores get so stupid? He was sure that they'd been able to outsmart him once upon a time, back when they still had power over him, before he became the man he was today. He slipped his hunting knife out of its sheath on his belt, and still, the stupid bitch didn't even shout for help. They were in the middle of a row of houses. All that they had to do to get rescued was to admit their weakness, to scream and scream for some man to come and save them.

It was their pride that had brought them to this. Strutting up and down the road in their high heels, with their short skirts. Never even turning their head when the good decent men across the way gave them a whistle of appreciation. Why couldn't they have just been good women? Kind, pure women. Richard knew that there was goodness in the world. He'd met his white angel, and she'd become the new standard by which all of these whores were judged. He didn't even notice the knife in his hand as he crouched down over her. He didn't even feel his pulse quicken as he laid a hand on her bare leg to draw her closer.

The front door banged open. Mary Ann and Suzanne had been out with some of the other nurses from their shift, chatting and drinking coffee to create a little buffer between the hospital and their home life. They came tumbling into the townhouse with a burst of giggles. They were exhausted after a long shift, but at least it was over now, and they had time to rest and recuperate. They were so drowsy that they'd made it almost to the bedroom at the back of the house before they saw that the door to the side was open, and there was a man with a knife hanging over Pamela's bound body. With a yelp, they fled through the house. There was some noise in the back bedroom, some voice speaking softly, so that was where they ran first. When the door opened, and they saw the other women, their closest friends, all bound up and arrayed across the floor, they screamed.

A strong hand clamped over Suzanne's face and dragged her back into the hall. Richard's other arm encircled Mary Ann and hauled her out, too, though he couldn't take a grip on her with his knife in hand. In the bedroom, the girls started screaming. Begging him not to hurt them. Begging them not to fight back. They went straight back down the hall, then staggered through into another bedroom. As the girls twisted and spun in his grasp, the door was slammed shut behind them. His hand over Suzanne's face was locked in place, pinning her mouth and nose shut but otherwise forgotten as Richard tried to fend off Mary Ann. Finally, a bitch with some fight in her. Finally, an excuse to cut loose. He hammered the knife into her stomach and delighted in the warm rush of blood over his knuckles. No part of a woman was ever so warm as when he made his own hole in her. No pleasure any woman could give would ever be as sweet as that little gasp she made when she realised that her life was over, and it was all because of him. Because he was more powerful than her. Because he'd decided that her life should end at this moment.

The other whore was still clawing at his hand as her friend collapsed in a heap, still braying like a donkey and bucking as if her feeble woman's body could ever overpower him. He dropped the knife on the dead one and fell on Suzanne with both arms outstretched. He rode her down onto an unmade bed in this den of sin and let his other hand slip into its natural place around her throat. When he whispered, it was so softly that even the woman bleeding out on the floor couldn't hear him. 'That's it. Fight me. Do it'.

Suzanne tried. She tried to push him off. She tried to buck her hips to shift the awful weight grinding down between her legs. She tried to bite the soft fleshy parts of his fingers where they were stretched over her lips and to pry his fingers apart. It was all for nothing. The strength was already leaving her. It'd been a full minute since she last drew breath, and already her lungs were burning. As her struggles weakened, Richard took his hand from her face and squeezed it around her neck alongside the other, not just pinching off the air supply, but crushing the soft tissues. Grinding the tiny, fragile parts of her throat together beneath his palms. She stopped breathing, she stopped moving, but still, Richard squeezed. He'd seen men choked out in bar fights before. He knew how long you had to suffocate somebody before they died, and it was a damn sight longer than the movies had people believing.

When he was finally satisfied that they were dead, he cleaned off his knife on their clothes, slipped it back into his belt and went to wash up. From the back bedroom, nobody could see the dead nurses. For all that they knew, the women were just bound and gagged. That was good. He didn't want to spoil anybody's surprise.

Once the initial rush of the murder passed him by, it was very much like the heroin all over again. Life crept back in, inch by inch. He had too many choices at the moment. He needed to narrow things down. Lumbering from room to room as the captured nurses wept, he found the bathroom and cleaned himself up so that the blood on his hands faded to little more than a rusty tint. Staring at his pallid face in the mirror, Richard could see his lips moving, but he had to strain to hear what he was saying aloud. 'Keep them calm, keep things easy. Enjoy yourself'.

Pamela was still alone in the bedroom where he'd left her, just calling out for attention, randomly selected for his pleasure. When he finally got back to her and saw her cowering there like a rabbit in the headlights of a truck, she abruptly lost all of her appeal. The other girls had some fire in them — they bucked and fought; they squirmed around in fascinating ways. This one was a wet fish, just lying there with tears leaking down her face. Richard rolled her onto her back with a kick, then straddled her waist, feeling her bound hands twitching against the underside of his erection as he ground against her. Pathetic. He didn't even try to hide the knife as he brought it up, and he certainly didn't give her the clean, violent death he'd given Mary Ann, who'd at least had the courage to fight him.

For the first time in his life, he had a woman's body laid out beneath him with no consequences to his actions. He had come completely untethered from the reality of the world outside of this house by now. This townhouse was the whole world, and he was its god. He put the tip of his knife to Pamela's chest, and he pushed down slowly, feeling the resistance of her skin, of the layers of fat and muscle. Feeling the glancing scrape of the ribcage, then the effortless hollow space of the heart. He slipped the knife back and forth a few times, in and out, just for the feel of it. When Pamela died, there was no ecstatic rush. He didn't even notice her passing away beneath him. She didn't struggle, even then. He stabbed her a few more times, tied one of her white stockings around her throat, as he would most of the girls when he was done with them. He liked the look of it.

Another trip to the bathroom dealt with the worst of the arterial spray that had caught him, and before too long, he was ready to return to the bedroom and pick his next victim. Even with the heroin easing his conscience, he'd been holding himself back before, certain that the world would rebel against him if he started acting solely for his own pleasure. His Christian upbringing had been at work, but now evidence had replaced philosophy. Nobody was stopping him. Nobody was even trying to stop him. Time to go back to the buffet.

The girls were trying their best to crawl away from him as he entered the room, wriggling like worms across the floor. That was good. That was how it should be. They were worms to him. They should be afraid. For some reason, his eyes locked on Nina, and he untied her legs so that she could get up and move around without assistance. 'I just want to talk to her right now. Not the rest of you. Just her. All right?'

Any trust he might have built up with the girls had crumbled in the face of his brutality towards the late arrivals. They were all terrified of him now. All of them shied away from his touch, and not one of them believed him when he said that he wasn't going to do them any harm. He didn't care. He had total control over everything now. Why would he care how they felt about it? If they were calm, that made life easier. If they went wild, then he could go just as wild in response.

It took a little tug on her hair, but Nina followed Richard out of the bedroom and down the hall to one of the few remaining empty bedrooms. 'I ain't going to hurt you, just lie yourself down'.

Nina was shaking all over as she tried to obey him. The tremors set the bed springs squeaking in gentle harmony. He leaned over her with a reassuring smile on his face, and despite everything she'd seen and heard, for one moment, Nina believed everything was going to be all right. Then, he pressed the pillow down onto her face. The moment that the illusion broke, all of the nervous energy vibrating away inside of Nina was unleashed in a fury. She flailed at Richard, landing a couple of good backhanded slaps on his face with her bound hands, sharp sounds in the sudden silence. They didn't hurt Richard, not exactly, but heat rose up where she had struck him, and soon the little bedroom felt like a furnace for her many haphazard attacks. He'd thought that smothering would be painless for her, that it would be easier for him with his hands still strained from choking the last whore to death, but this was taking far too long. The bed had too much bounce to it, and she was able to snatch gasps of air as she squirmed away from him.

Richard drew the knife. He tugged away the pillow and jabbed the blade into her neck. It wasn't a clean, killing blow. He missed the arteries, slicing into her throat instead, leaving her gurgling and choking on her own blood as she still struggled to push him off, as if anything could save her now. He stabbed into her neck, again and again, pulling her nightdress up so that he could see her naked breasts heaving as she choked and spluttered. Despite her weakness, he allowed her to push him back. He stepped down off the bed and backed away towards the door. Without his weight to hold her down, the girl humped and heaved on the bed, struggling as if there was some invisible force still pressing down against her. Nina let out another gurgling gasp, spraying the top half of the bed with the blood bubbling up from between her lips, then she lay still. She had choked on her own blood. Richard crept in closer to take a better look and clean off his knife. He gave her a couple of prods, just to be sure she was dead. She was.

Almost out of habit more than any desire to maintain appearances, Richard dawdled back through to the bathroom and cleaned himself off. The girls were wailing as they heard him going back and forth, knowing that any one of them could be next. This was the life. This was how it should always have been. The women cowering in terror as a man stood proudly over them, doing whatever he saw fit. This would teach all of those whores around the world a lesson. This was their place, and they'd all see that by the time he was done. The other men would learn their lesson, too. They'd see what he had done here and realise that they didn't have to be slaves to the whores. They could overcome their power. Men could set aside their desperate hunger for that slippery thing they kept locked between their legs and seek out the higher pleasure. The hotter holes that Richard and his knife so eagerly made.

When he got back into the bedroom, he let out a little bark of laughter. The girls had tried to wriggle under the beds as if that would be enough to keep them safe. One had her head wedged between the metal and the carpet and was letting out a steady whine. Richard grabbed her by the ankle and tugged to free her, and that just set her off bawling and sobbing. Pathetic.

Valentina was up next. He didn't even bother to untie her legs. She was a tiny woman who weighed less than 100 pounds. He could have juggled with her if he wanted.

The remaining women didn't know what fate awaited them. They lay as still as they could and strained their hearing, trying to work out what Richard would do to them next. The only exception was Corazon, the girl who'd first opened the door to him. She was determined to do something, anything, to get out of her situation. It was her head that Richard had released from where she'd wedged it under the bed frame, and now she set about wriggling underneath the other bunk bed instead. She'd dealt with plenty of drug-seeking addicts in her time at the hospital. She recognised the symptoms — Richard's blown-out pupils, his pallid skin, the sweating. He was on something, and that meant that his perceptions were altered. If she could just get out of sight, the drug-addled maniac might just pass her over. She hadn't come all the way around the world on some reeking tanker ship just to die here now that she'd finally arrived in America. She was going to live. She had to live.

It felt like her head was being crushed by the pressure, but she managed to get it past the bedframe. Yet, even she paused when she heard Valentina cry out in pain. Even she stopped her desperate writhing when she heard the tap in the bathroom turn on once again. He was washing his hands clean of them, one at a time.

Merlita was the next woman to die. Another exchange student from the Philippines, here to improve herself. To help save lives. Richard grabbed her by her bound wrists and lifted her body off the floor. Her feet dangled beneath her like she was a ragdoll. That was all that they were to Richard, meat dolls that he could play with and discard.

Cora had been studying him throughout this whole ordeal, hunting for some sign of weakness to exploit. She could see that he wasn't a bulky man, but he had wiry strength enough for these impressive feats hidden beneath his plain black clothes. Any hope of overpowering him and escaping faded as he strolled out of the room with the shrieking Merlita still hanging from one hand, bare toes trailing the carpet like she was a sack of groceries. This time, Cora didn't pause. She pressed and wriggled deeper and deeper under the bed until she was pressed up against the wall and could go no further. For a long moment, there was no sound outside of her own frantic breathing. Then she heard Merlita's voice, as soft as a whisper through the wall. It was like she was speaking only to Cora. 'Masakit'. A Filipino word that meant 'it hurts'.

A few minutes later, the water was turned on again. Whatever he'd done to Merlita, whatever had drawn out that word from across the world, it was over now. Her pain was over now. It was a small comfort as Cora lay there, curled up around herself, praying for this hell to end.

Pat Matusek was the next victim, one that Richard had been saving for a special treat. She was an athletic woman of about 150 pounds, well-muscled and liable to put up a fight. She reminded him of the bartender he used to babysit for. That bitch who'd chased him away the minute he showed he was a man, not some whipped dog. Pat was the one that had first turned his head, the reason that he decided to stake this place out and rob it — just for the chance to get his hands on her, to feel the strength in her limbs and prove beyond any doubt that he was stronger. He was more powerful. He could do what he wanted. He'd seen Pat walking down the street, softness and hardness together, her sculpted body beneath a flowing yellow sundress. It'd stirred his attentions the way that few of these other nurses ever had. He wanted her. He wanted to prove himself to her so badly; it left him aching.

The others he'd taken to the bedrooms, but now he was running out of places to kill them. He led Pat in shuffling steps through to the bathroom. Exhaustion and arousal washed over him in waves. The drugs and the ecstatic rush of the killing drained even his boundless strength away, and the room seemed to swim around them. He stared at her hard once they were in the bathroom, squinting in the dim light to try and see her properly as his eyes slipped in and out of focus. 'Are you the girl in the yellow dress?'

He hadn't meant to speak, but the same barriers that kept him from acting out his brutal impulses held back every thought that sprang into his head, and they'd been thoroughly demolished by this night's activities.

'Are you?'

He stumbled towards her, and Pat managed to catch the edge of the sink behind her back to stop that sudden lunge from toppling her to the tiles. His vision swam again. Shirley Ann's face stared out at him from the dark. Then that bitch bartender. Then his mother. Martha. All of the women, blending and twisting, all of them looking down on him. Pat's face came up out of the morass, her lip twisted up in disgust. Her loathing for him obvious. Like she was better than him. Like any of those whores were better than him. He hammered his fist into her guts. Practice made perfect, and even addled as he was, it followed the same murderous trajectory as the last time he'd thrown a punch. Mary Kay Pierce, the last woman to look at him like that — her sneering face danced over Pat's before the woman collapsed. On the ground, she looked different again, smaller somehow. She was all curled up around herself, retching and twitching as her ruptured liver killed her. Her flushed face turned pale, and on the sterile white tile, she looked like someone else entirely. She wasn't the woman in the yellow dress. She was his white angel, his Judy. He'd killed Judy. The one good woman in all the world, and he'd hammered his fist into her guts and burst her. In the mirror, he could see his lips moving again, but he had to lean his forehead right up against the cold glass to hear his own words. 'It isn't her'.

He looked down again, and the bitch, the bartender, the wrestler, the mother-wife-sister whore who deserved nothing more than death, was lying at his feet. Not his angel. Just Pat, the girl in the yellow dress. He let out a gasp of relief. All was well.

He washed the blood from his hands and headed back to the bedroom. There was only one of the whores left. He'd burned through all the rest so quickly he could hardly believe how easy it'd been. He counted them off on his fingers — this one made eight. Still, this one was the vilest and whorish of the lot. He'd dumped her on the one low bed in the room after she'd come staggering in reeking of liquor and men, obviously just finished selling herself to whoever came along. To add insult to injury, she'd fallen asleep while he was off killing all the rest of her whore friends.

He'd killed seven women. The thought reverberated around in the dark hollow of his skull. Seven of them. Without even having to try. All this time, he'd been so afraid, and there was no need. They were soft and tempting, but they were dreadfully feeble creatures for all of the power that they wielded. This would be the eighth one. The eighth of the whores that lived in this house. The worst of the worst, pretending to be angels like his Judy, while they were whores. This whore was the worst of them all, and she was sleeping like a baby. It wasn't right.

He tore open her dress and buttons scattered across the room, a few even making it as far as Cora where she was huddled under the bed, staring out in horror as Richard stripped one of her dearest friends of her clothes and dignity. He struggled for a moment with Gloria's underwear before drawing out his knife and cutting right through the elastic and underwire.

Cora wanted to look away. She wanted to hide her face, cover her ears and pretend that what she could see right in front of her wasn't happening, but fear had paralysed her. She lay under the bed and watched as Richard mounted Gloria while he raped her.

After a minute or so, he became more vigorous, and Gloria stirred from her alcohol-infused coma to scream. She tried to pull her legs together, tried to bat him away, but he pressed the knife to her neck and just kept on pounding on. He leaned down close to her face, a feral grin locked on his features.

He leaned so close to Gloria that Cora was afraid that he would see her hiding there under the bed. She couldn't move for fear of him hearing her, but all it would take would be a glance in her direction, and she would die.

He got faster and rougher again. Gloria's head lolled to the side, and Cora could see the tears flowing down her expressionless face. Gloria had gone away somewhere inside her own head, somewhere that she could escape the horrors that were happening around her.

Cora envied her that, envied that she could escape from this nightmare even if it was only into the embrace of madness. There would be no such luck for Corazon. Richard's whole body arched back, and he let out a howl as he finished his filthy work. Cora took that moment to squeeze herself even closer to the wall and squeeze her eyes shut. If he was coming for her, she didn't want to know about it. She worried that the fear alone might make her cry out, so she took her lips between her teeth and bit down until they were bloody. She would stay there, curled up under the bed until it was all over.

With a grunt of effort, Richard rolled off Gloria and tucked his withering manhood back into his trousers. The whole night had been a build-up to that sweet release, and now he found himself quite exhausted. Even disposing of this last one seemed like too much effort. He stumbled to his feet, took hold of her ankle bindings and pulled, dragging her through the hallway like a piece of furniture. She was so far gone that she didn't even make a sound of complaint. In the living room, he draped her over one of the seats and took a moment to admire her. This was the kind of woman that would never have given him the time of day if he'd approached her in the street, and now she was his to do whatever he pleased with. He cupped one of her breasts as his hands and gaze travelled up the length of her body, but by now, all of the appeal had fled her. Just another whore to dispose of. There was a spare length of torn sheet tucked in his belt. He drew it out between his hands and then wrapped it around Gloria's neck.

He'd never used a ligature to choke a woman before. All of his previous strangulations had been by hand with the stocking tied around as an afterthought. He had no idea how hard he had to pull. He had no idea how deeply a band of twisted cloth would bite into the woman's neck. He twisted the cord around with all of his strength, pulling it tighter and tighter even as it cut into his hands. Gloria made a few involuntary jerks, but all the fight had already been knocked out of her. She was dead inside long before he decided to choke her out. Even when it was over, the cloth stayed tight inside her neck, with flesh overlapping it on both sides. One final act of brutal overkill.

Finally, it was all over. The greatest night of Richard's life. He washed himself off one last time, taking care to step around the body on the floor. He paused by the front door and looked back into the house, counting down in his head. Eight student nurses lived here, and eight women had died at his hands. His work here was done, and the whole world of whores would remember. He slipped out the front door. The house fell silent.

The Horror and the Hunt

At five o'clock in the morning, a beeping alarm woke Judy Dykton with a groan. She had a neurology exam later in the day and needed to do some last-minute cramming if she wanted to pass. The sweltering July heat had her running a fan all night long, much to the chagrin of the Filipino exchange students that shared housing with her, but she switched it off when she got to her desk as the buzzing sound was distracting her. There was an even more distracting noise outside, something like an animal cry, repeating over and over. Judy rolled her eyes. No way was she getting any reading done with that going on. She grabbed some laundry and headed downstairs. Hopefully, whatever creature was so miserable out there would be done by the time that the wash cycle was set up. On her return to her bedroom, the plaintive wailing had gotten louder. It sounded like it was coming from right outside her window. She strolled over and opened the blinds to the dawn's red rays. That was when she saw Corazon.

Across the road at 2319, Cora had crawled out onto a window-ledge overlooking the street, and she was bawling her eyes out. It sent a chill up Judy's spine. Some of the girls were prone to dramatics. Some of them might have taken a break-up hard and acted out like that, but not Cora, never Cora. She had her head on straight. Wrapping a robe around herself, Judy rushed down the stairs and across the empty road. Cora's sobbing was unrelenting. 'They're all dead. Oh my God. They're all dead'.

Judy only made it up the first flight of stairs before the truth of Cora's wailing was revealed. The door to the living room hung open, and there was Gloria, spread-eagled naked across the sofa with some sort of cord wrapped around her neck so tight it looked like her head was liable to pop right off. She was already turning blue. Without a moment's pause, Judy sprinted back to her own house and woke all her fellow students and the house mother for the street of students, Mrs Bisone. They returned to 2319 in a huge group, clustered together despite the already rising temperature. Just as they were about to step inside, Cora jumped down onto the steps in front of them. 'No!'

She stumbled to her feet and grabbed at the closest nurses. 'Don't go in. He might still be in there. Don't go. Everyone on the sampan has been killed. Everyone'.

The word of one girl was not enough for Mrs Bisone. She'd suffered through years of students' practical jokes and mental breakdowns — she wouldn't believe what was being said until she saw it with her own eyes. Room by room, they moved through the townhouse, pausing at each dead body for Mrs Bisone to bark out their surname, as if they might snap to attention. Not one of them stirred. It was true. They were all dead. Every last girl, except for Cora.

Mrs Bisone snatched up the phone and called the hospital. 'All of my girls have been murdered'.

The receptionist asked, 'Who has been killed?'

'I don't know. I... I need help.' She hung up and ran outside to be sick. It fell to the other girls who were now close to hysterics to flag down a police car.

Daniel Kelly had only been on the police force for a year and a half. He was in no way equipped for what he was about to see in the townhouse that he drew up to, surrounded by sobbing women. Informed by the chorus of wailing voices that there'd been a murder, he drew his gun and went inside. He found Gloria first and almost immediately fled. He'd dated Gloria's sister for a few months; he knew her. He could still hear her voice echoing in his head as he looked at her naked, raped body, sprawled out and turning purple. Gritting his teeth, he managed to search through the rest of the house, confirming that the killer had left the building before he returned to his car and radioed for immediate assistance. 'They are dead. They're all dead. Oh God. Give me the sergeant. I dated her sister. Oh God. I've never seen anything like this'.

The reinforcements that Officer Kelly called were dispatched, but they were not the next to arrive on the scene. Crime reporter Joe Cummings had been doing his early morning tour of the local stations, hunting for gossip when he picked up Kelly's report on his radio. Most of what he heard was just gibberish about everybody being dead, but in amongst that macabre chatter, he managed to catch the address, and he tore over there as fast as his old car could go. He snatched up his tape recorder and darted out into the street.

Kelly had his gun still in hand, and he raised it as Joe approached. 'Whoa there. I'm with you. I'm a police reporter. Joe Cummings with WCFL. What happened here?'

'Homicide', Kelly managed to mumble out. He was really shaken. Joe could see that something big was going on — even rookies didn't get this freaked out over a corpse or two.

'I'm just going to take a look inside. I ain't going to touch anything. All right?'

Still lost in his own thoughts, Kelly just nodded.

Stepping inside, Cummings saw Gloria's body almost immediately. He called out, 'You've got one in the living room'. He couldn't understand what all the fuss was about. The naked dame looked a bit nasty, but this was very much a run of the mill homicide.

Kelly called back, 'Keep looking'.

One by one, Cummings uncovered the bodies. Whispering notes to himself about the ochre colour of their flesh, the positioning of the corpses, the casual disposal of the bodies. By the time that he got back outside, he was repeating the same mantra as Kelly, over and over. 'Oh my god. Oh my god'.

By the time that the rest of the police arrived in force, Joe was over by the bushes throwing up. A few of the officers laughed at him, mocking his weak guts in the face of a body or two. He just shook his head at them. They'd see. They'd all see.

Kelly had gone to join Cora in the other house, where she was encircled by her friends, desperately clinging to the last shreds of her sanity after what she'd witnessed. A doctor from the hospital had arrived and was administering a sedative to the girl by the time Joe got his head back in order and tried to get on with his job. He followed Cora's steady wailing to the other townhouse and asked who she was. 'A survivor'.

'Where does she live?'

'She was visiting from next door'.

When Joe emerged, he headed over to his car to radio in a report for the six-a.m. news. He'd covered plane crashes before, where body parts were strewn for miles, but he'd never seen anything like this. As he watched, the cops who'd been mocking him for his weak stomach came rushing out of the house to add to the gathering pool of vomit by the storm drain. He gave a basic report: eight student nurses murdered in a spree, more details to follow.

Frank Flanagan was the commander of Chicago City's homicide unit. He cornered Joe at about six o'clock in the morning to dictate the terms of his coverage. Nothing was to be mentioned about the way that the girls were killed. Nothing was to be said beyond them having their throats cut. The sexual assaults, the intricate patterns of stab wounds and the stockings were all to be held back. The police didn't want every weirdo in the city calling up to lay claim to these murders, burning through all of the resources that they needed to turn on the real perpetrator. Joe was happy to oblige. He was going to have nightmares about this killing spree for the rest of his life — he wanted the perpetrator caught.

Officials from the nursing school were brought in to identify the bodies. Cora had already been taken off for observation at the hospital, and nobody wanted to force her to relive the horrors of the night before again when she was so fragile. The neighbours managed to identify a few of the girls, the head of nursing a few more, and eventually, the whole lot were turned over to the coroner. Eight dead girls in all. He checked them all over for the signs of their injuries and causes of death, noted the way that their clothing had been disturbed, their pubic hair and breasts exposed, even when there was no further sign of sexual assault. Finally, he carted the bodies out, hidden from the prying eyes of the gathered public and sealed the house. That was when the forensics specialists were finally unleashed.

Meanwhile, police fanned out through the local streets, hunting for anyone that matched Cora's faltering description. The gas station attendant who'd held Richard's bags remembered him, though he didn't know his name. Despite that, he did recall Richard's grumbling about missing out on a sailing job due to a double-booking. That, in turn, led the police to the NMU hiring hall. One of the union guys remembered a blonde with a southern accent so thick he could barely understand him, but he couldn't recall his name. Luckily, the police and the union were able to find the paperwork from the double-booking that Richard had been complaining about in the waste-paper bin behind the counter.

The fingerprints, photograph and physical description from the Coastguard's registration documents matched with Cora's description and the prints found in bloody handprints at the scene of the crime. Richard Speck was positively identified as the killer they were looking for within hours. It was a spectacular piece of good old-fashioned police work, but it still wasn't enough. They didn't just have to identify their murderer; they had to find him before he could kill again.

From the scene of his greatest accomplishment, Richard had headed back to the Shipyard Inn, where he'd washed himself off in the communal bathroom and headed to bed. The next morning, he woke up feeling sprightly with his newly refilled wallet. He headed down to meet some drinking buddies at Pete's Tap at about half-past ten. In all of their time together, his friends had never seen him looking better. Weeks back, Richard had pawned his watch to the bartender in exchange for some more bourbon, but now he had ready cash to buy it back and a round for his friends. It raised a few eyebrows. Richard was never that well off, or that generous.

Hooking up with his buddies Robert 'Red' Gerald and William Kirkland, he continued to drink his way through the day. It was in the Soko-Grad that Richard heard the news that there was a survivor of his massacre, but he was quick to deflect attention, casually saying, 'Must have been some dirty motherfucker that done it,' before moving on with bragging about the hooker he'd taken back to his room yesterday who had such a good time she gave him a freebie. Red was a fellow country boy, but unlike Richard, he hadn't spent his whole life drinking like a fish. By late afternoon he was a wreck, so Richard took him back to his room in the Shipyard Inn to sleep it off.

Richard himself headed down to the bar because he had a phone call. It was his brother-in-law, Gene. Apparently, the union hall had a berth for him; he just needed to come in to pick it up. It was perfect. Richard was well aware that Chicago was going to go berserk in the hunt for whoever killed those nurses, and this was the perfect opportunity to get out of the way of the impending manhunt. He wasn't desperate for money, but despite his lack of self-reflection, even he knew that his usual habits would burn through the takings from the townhouse robbery in no time at all. Still, the call raised some questions. After his long days of lingering in the hall, Richard knew that the

NMU didn't call you up with work, and he sincerely doubted that Gene had been hanging around the hall for him. He rang into the NMU hall to ask about the job rather than heading there himself and found the usually surly staff to be bizarrely helpful. There was a berth just waiting for him on the Sinclair Great Lakes. All he had to do was come down to the hall and pick up the papers. Richard made a big fuss of his excitement about the new job, but once the call was over, he headed upstairs to wake Red and pack his bags. The Sinclair Great Lakes had shipped out three days ago, and the police would be tracing the call back to this flophouse. He needed to get the hell out of town.

While they waited for a taxi to arrive, Red sat out on the curb, still trying to recover from his day's drinking while Richard played pool by himself in the back of the bar. As he waited, three plainclothes policemen from the taskforce showed up asking for 'a tall blond man with a southern accent', but the bartender elected not to give up one of his best customers. The police departed empty-handed, and Richard left a hefty tip as he headed out to get his taxi.

After dropping off Red, Richard took a trip to the 'beatnik' part of town, near the Cabrini-Green projects, moving swiftly through the clean streets, feeling the scrutiny of passers-by. He found what he was looking for swiftly. The Raleigh Hotel had fallen from its former glory into just another cheap flophouse. He spent that first night in the company of a local black prostitute, who was sure to stop by reception and warn the girl behind the counter that Richard had a gun.

The police were called in and confiscated the pistol from the man, but even though they looked at his identification and paperwork, the details of the townhouse murders hadn't been disseminated to the police force at large. They left Richard to go on about his business.

By this time, the police had followed Richard's trail and gotten hold of Red, pumping him for any information about Richard's movements. They picked up the taxi driver from the previous day and then spread armed officers all around Cabrini-Green, just waiting for Speck to show his face.

Now realising that the Raleigh Hotel wouldn't hide him, Richard relocated to the Starr Hotel, the cheapest place that he'd ever stayed in, with plain concrete cells and chicken-wire in place of walls and windows. His timing was impeccable yet again. The taskforce of plainclothes officers showed up at his previous hotel with a mugshot, and he was immediately identified by the receptionist. They knew that he was close, but they had no idea how close.

Richard met up with a pair of travelling hobos called 'One-Eye' and 'Shorty', sharing a bottle of wine with them and trying to learn the best place to hop a train out of town. The homeless alcoholics soon began to feel that something was off with the man they were sharing their boardings with and did their best to lose him, leaving Richard alone with his thoughts.

The next day, he managed to track One-Eye down again, demanding that he take him out of town immediately, but the homeless man had no intention of leaving Chicago any time soon. There was day work here for him and liquor as far as the eye could see. Disgusted and disappointed, Richard set off to skid row to pawn some of his sparse belongings for some drinking money. He stopped by a liquor store on his way back to the hotel to pick up a bottle of wine, and there, he was frozen in place. His face was plastered over the front of every single newspaper. Row after row of them. All glaring out at him. His name was right there beside the pictures. The whole world would know him now. The whole world would be looking. All his life he'd claimed that he was born to raise hell, but now that he'd actually done it, he was terrified of what was going to happen next. He rushed back to the hotel, forced his way into One-Eye's room and started to guzzle the wine. Meanwhile, One-Eye headed down to the payphones outside to call the police tip line. Richard Speck was in his hotel room, after all. The police opted to ignore this rambling drunk's call, allowing the events that followed to happen.

With the wine finished, Richard smashed the bottle on the cot's metal frame and slashed his wrists all the way up to the elbow before collapsing on the cold concrete floor. The police may not have come, but an ambulance arrived shortly, taking him off to Cook County Hospital. The same hospital where the bodies of his victims were being autopsied at that very moment.

If he'd hoped that he would awaken surrounded by beautiful white-clad angels again, he was sorely mistaken. His wrists were all bound up in bandages, but over the top of them were a pair of handcuffs. The junior doctor who'd performed his initial diagnosis recognised the 'Born to Raise Hell' tattoo from the news reports and called in the police before taking the man off to surgery for a severed artery.

The Last Whore

The state's attorney, William Martin, parked himself outside of Speck's door from the moment he was wheeled upstairs. There was no way that he was going to allow anyone to speak to the man while he was under the influence of painkillers, as that could be used as an argument against the veracity of his statements. Martin had taken full control over the case against Speck from the very start and was fighting a dozen running battles to keep Cora Amurao out of the reach of the press and even the Philippine government. He put up his eye witness in an apartment under 24-hour guard and even flew in her mother to give her some comfort. Throughout the whole thing, he treated her with kid gloves, terrified that she might break under the mental strain of what she'd been through and leave him without a witness to pin everything on Speck.

After several days, Martin was confronted with a dilemma. If he could get Cora to make a positive identification of Speck now, he wouldn't have to rely on her so heavily in court — he could just take in a signed affidavit of her statement if she was snatched up by some foreign power or broken by the pressure. Against all of his instincts, he had Cora brought to the hospital dressed in her own nurse's uniform. She walked around for a while with one of her friends, as though they were just doing rounds, then she came into Richard's room.

She stared at the sedated man for a few minutes before quietly shuffling outside to collapse in the arms of Martin and the detectives, crushed under the weight of her memories. 'It's really him'.

The forensic evidence that'd been collected at the scene of the crime was combined with clothing of Speck's that was found abandoned and bloodstained. A history of the man was developed, and ties to his previous crimes were discovered. Fingerprints were everywhere, smeared in the blood of Richard's victims. 133 pages of testimony were gathered from Cora, detailing every single event in order, right up until the moment that the police arrived. Richard himself was finally weaned off the drugs for long enough to give his own statement, claiming to remember nothing about the night in question, even though, in an addled state shortly after his surgery, he had blithely discussed the details of his wholesale slaughter with one of his doctors, thinking that it was already all over.

The public defender assigned to Speck was Gerald Getty, and in all of his life, Richard had never been so lucky as to end up in that man's care. Getty hammered the prosecution with motion after motion and managed to have vital evidence excluded. The pistol that Richard had used was seized in an illegal search. The testimony of the prostitute who saw it was suspect. The bloody t-shirts that had been found on his case may have been stained when one of the investigating officers snagged himself on the case. The reliability of almost every witness who'd spent time with Richard after the crime was committed was drawn into question by the sheer volume of liquor they'd imbibed. Everywhere the prosecution turned, they hit another roadblock.

Getty also hit the prosecution with more interference beyond the evidence, arguing that there was no possible way for Richard to receive a fair trial in Chicago when the police had plastered his face across every newspaper, labelling him a murderer before any proof had even been given. His final piece of legal trickery was a masterstroke, arguing that the sentence that any jury handed down for any one of the individual murders would be unduly influenced by the knowledge of any of the other seven. If this motion had carried, then eight separate trials would have had to be conducted for that one night of terror, with a new jury each time made up of people with no knowledge of Richard's prior convictions. An impossibility. If the judge had allowed it, then it would've guaranteed Richard a mistrial and his freedom.

Judge Paschen allowed the vast majority of the motions but blocked the final one. Evidence would be excluded, and the trial relocated, but all eight murders would be tried together, and despite the trial being moved several miles south to Peoria, Paschen himself would still preside over it to ensure consistency.

Throughout all of this, Getty was cycling through dozens of psychiatric experts, trying to get at least one who would state that Richard was clinically insane and couldn't be held responsible for his actions during the night in question. Examination revealed that Richard's brain was malformed due to his head injury, with the parts relating to emotional control being compromised and the line between rational and irrational thoughts blurred. Still, it wasn't enough to prove he wasn't competent to stand trial. Others believed that Richard was a sociopath, but that wasn't sufficient either. One of the psychologists, the regular at the jail where he was being held, a Dr Ziporyn, believed Richard's defence. He provided a diagnosis of depression, anxiety and an obsessive-compulsive personality — all traits associated with drug addiction and withdrawal — while also noting the great love that Richard claimed to hold for his family. But even Ziporyn couldn't overlook the Madonna/whore complex that dominated the man's psychology. It was impossible to make it through a page of notes relating to Richard without him referring to women in a derogatory fashion. Even when he was talking about events that had nothing to do with the women in his life, his talking therapy always circled back to them and tried to place the blame for his actions on their doorstep. Even in the run-up to the trial, he blamed his ex-wife for his actions, claiming that he had no intention of doing anything but robbing the townhouse until the first nurse opened the door and looked just like her.

Turning to the new science of genetics, Getty communicated with a Swiss endocrinologist who believed that Richard may have been born with the uncommon XYY karyotype, something that at the time was believed to cause carriers to grow to at least 6 foot tall, overdevelop musculature and develop the kind of mental disabilities that would make it impossible for them to tell right from wrong. As it turned out, Richard was not XYY, and the characterisation of XYY people as aggressive, violent criminals was disproved with a very small amount of additional research.

The next step was the arduous process of jury selection. Even outside of Chicago it was practically impossible to find jurors who hadn't heard about Speck's crimes in gruesome, prejudicial detail. It took the court six weeks to draw a jury pool out of over 600 potential candidates.

Cora and her mother were snuck into town under cover of darkness, and the local Ramada Inn was filled to bursting with all of the players in Speck's story. Every witness to any part of his comings and goings surrounding the townhouse murders were sequestered there under the prosecution's watchful eyes.

Once the trial began on 3 April 1967, Gerald Getty tore through the evidence that the prosecution had provided. Even the fingerprints may have been interfered with, thanks to the reporter who'd blundered through the scene before it was locked down for forensic investigation. Getty strongly implied that the police were so desperate to find a scapegoat that they were framing Richard. All of the evidence presented against him fell apart — up until the moment that Cora took the stand.

With an almost impossible grace given the circumstances, Cora described the events of that night in perfect detail, finally coming down out of the witness box to point directly at Richard's face while declaring him the man who'd killed all of her friends. 'This is the man'. The whole courthouse fell deathly silent during her testimony, interrupted only by the sobbing of the parents of the victims as they heard the details of what had happened to their daughters.

It was enough. On the 15th of April, after only 49 minutes of deliberation, the jury came back with their findings. Speck was guilty of all eight murders, and he was sentenced to death. An immediate stay of execution was put in place so that the case could be examined by a higher court, but on 22nd November 1968, the Supreme Court of Illinois was happy to ratify that sentence.

As preparations were made for Richard to be executed by the electric chair, there were further examinations of his case, and on 28 June 1971, the Supreme Court ruled that he must be granted another sentence after it was discovered that over 200 potential jurors were excluded by the prosecution because they held religious or moral views against capital punishment.

On 21 November 1972, Richard was resentenced to a minimum of 400 years in prison. Parole hearings would come later in his life but rarely lasted more than 10 minutes before they were denied. The first was in 1976, but later ones took place in 1977, 1978, 1981, 1984, 1987 and 1990. It became apparent after a while that Richard was only applying for parole as something to do to keep himself amused. He had a long time to serve and very little to fill it with.

In Stateville Correctional Center in Crest Hill, Illinois, Richard kept a pair of sparrows as pets after they flew into his cell, nursing one of them back to health after it'd broken its wing. He'd never had pets in his early life, and here in prison, these little birds gave him the chance to exercise some control over another living thing in a way that wasn't immediately punished. Eventually, the warden himself came down to talk to him about his birds and let him know that they weren't permitted under the prison rules. Richard responded by throwing them into a fan, splattering the room with blood. If he couldn't have them, nobody could.

He ignored the rules whenever it suited him, spending all of his time pursuing the next high. Illicit moonshine and smuggled drugs were commonplace, and Richard traded off his fame to secure freebies as frequently as possible. When the guards challenged him, he just laughed, 'What are you going to do to me, lock me up for another thousand years?'

He denied media requests for the most part, with the exception of one newspaper columnist for the Chicago Tribune, to whom he granted a single interview. In that interview, he finally admitted to the murders, claimed that he had no feelings about the deaths that he'd caused, reiterated that he had no real memory of the events of the townhouse killings and explained his behaviour away as him being 'freakish'. Finally, he left a message for the families of the women he killed and the American people, telling them that their hatred was what kept him going. 'Just tell them to keep up their hatred for me. I know it keeps up their morale. And I don't know what I'd do without it'.

After that interview, Richard seemed to feel like his work was done, and his time in the spotlight was over. He slipped into the darkness of his cell and his own thoughts until the years stripped him of the strength that he used to lord over others. Day by day, new prisoners arrived in Stateville, people who'd grown up with stories about serial killers far more fearsome than Speck. All of the respect that he'd banked on began to fade away. All the strength that he used to get his way faded as he lounged around, his blond hair prematurely greying and his gut thickening.

It isn't immediately clear when Richard began prostituting himself for drugs and alcohol. Among the contraband that his clients smuggled in, were hormones that allowed Richard to develop breasts and silk underwear that he would parade around in during parties before servicing the other men. He'd finally found a relationship to women in his head that made sense. They could be outside of prison, pure and perfect, and inside, he could be the whore that he'd always accused them of being. He could soak up all of the hatred from the other men, latching onto them for all that he was worth.

A video would emerge of his activities in his later years, released to the public by some unknown amateur journalist within the prison. It showed Speck dancing in his underwear, snorting cocaine, fellating the other men and bragging to the camera about his crimes. When he was asked about how he felt about his time in prison, the former tough-guy mass-murderer descended into girlish giggles. 'If they knew how much fun I was having, they'd turn me loose!'

He'd become a caricature of the whores that he'd always imagined, and fulfilling that purpose seemed to bring him some measure of peace. He bore none of the usual markers for a transgender person, and indeed none of the many psychologists who studied him through the years had even considered it a possibility. This was not a switch of identity but an attempt to surface some deep-rooted belief from inside his twisted mind and give it a physical form. To him, the world was filled with whores, so here, in a place with no women, he had to create one out of the only flesh that he could manipulate.

Some have argued that the hormonal treatments, costumes and sexual exploitation were just punishments inflicted on Richard by the other inmates or the price that he had to pay to satisfy his addictions, but the Madonna/whore complex that dominated his psychology throughout his life would suggest otherwise. It may have started that way, but it seems likely that, in Speck's black-and-white worldview, there was only one place where he now fitted in. By the time that he was videotaped, there was no sign of duress in his manner or his actions. He was devoting himself body and soul to the role that he'd found.

On 5 December 1991, a day before his 50th birthday, that body gave out. A lifetime of drug abuse had ruined his heart, and he began experiencing stabbing pains in his chest that led to him being carted off to Silver Cross Hospital in Joliet, where he promptly died of a massive heart attack.

His haunting of the victim's families was at an end, and medical science finally had the chance to look at the physical brain deformation that their scans had so clearly demonstrated during his trial. The hippocampus, which is involved in memory, and the amygdala, which controls strong emotions like rage, were fused and blurred in a manner that was previously unknown to medical science. It was likely the result of the head injuries that Richard had suffered at the hands of his stepfather as a child, compounded by a lifetime of drug and alcohol abuse. Dr Leestma discovered these gross abnormalities at the Chicago Center for Neurosurgery and shipped off tissue slides to a colleague in Boston. Somewhere in transit, the pieces of the murderer's brain were stolen, presumably by a collector of serial killer memorabilia or a seller who could see the value in such grim trophies.

The rest of Richard's body wasn't claimed. His heart had occluded arteries and had enlarged to many times its original size. His once sleek, pockmarked face had become doughy as he packed on over 200 pounds in prison.

The coroner was able to contact his youngest sister, Carolyn, but she was doing all that she could to distance herself and her daughters from their murderous uncle. It was agreed that Richard was to be cremated and his remains scattered somewhere outside of the public eye. Neither the coroner nor Carolyn wanted there to be a grave for Richard. Neither of them wanted it to become a place of pilgrimage for the sick and twisted or an opportunity for further desecration.

His remains were cast into the wind, and some prayers were spoken softly, exactly the kind of ceremony he would've hated. Then he was gone.

The torment didn't end for the families of his victims, even with his death. Year after year, the press came around again, begging for interviews and insights. Year after year, new films and songs and books about Speck came out, reminding everyone of that one, nightmarish night all over again.

The videotape of him having the time of his life in prison surfaced in 1996 — five years after his death — and it received a public showing that scarred all of the viewers with his callous disregard for the women he'd killed. In that video, all that he had to say about them in terms of why he'd killed and raped them when he could've just committed his burglary and moved on unnoticed was this — 'It just wasn't their night'.

Want More?

Did you enjoy *The Townhouse Massarce* and want some more True Crime?

YOUR FREE BOOK IS WAITING

From bestselling author Ryan Green

There is a man who is officially classed as **"Britain's most dangerous prisoner"**

The man's name is Robert Maudsley, and his crimes earned him the nickname **"Hannibal the Cannibal"**

This free book is an exploration of his story...

★★★★★ *"Ryan brings the horrifying details to life. I can't wait to read more by this author!"*

Get a free copy of ***Robert Maudsley: Hannibal the Cannibal*** when you sign up to join my Reader's Group.

www.ryangreenbooks.com/free-book

Every Review Helps

If you enjoyed the book and have a moment to spare, I would really appreciate a short review on Amazon. Your help in spreading the word is gratefully received and reviews make a huge difference to helping new readers find me. Without reviewers, us self-published authors would have a hard time!

Type in your link below to be taken straight to my book review page.

US	geni.us/townhouseUS
UK	geni.us/townhouseUK
Australia	geni.us/townhouseAUS
Canada	geni.us/townhouseCA

Thank you! I can't wait to read your thoughts.

About Ryan Green

Ryan Green is a true crime author who lives in Herefordshire, England with his wife, three children, and two dogs. Outside of writing and spending time with his family, Ryan enjoys walking, reading and windsurfing.

Ryan is fascinated with History, Psychology and True Crime. In 2015, he finally started researching and writing his own work and at the end of the year, he released his first book on Britain's most notorious serial killer, Harold Shipman.

He has since written several books on lesser-known subjects, and taken the unique approach of writing from the killer's perspective. He narrates some of the most chilling scenes you'll encounter in the True Crime genre.

You can sign up to Ryan's newsletter to receive a free book, updates, and the latest releases at:

WWW.RYANGREENBOOKS.COM

More Books by Ryan Green

In July 1965, teenagers Sylvia and Jenny Likens were left in the temporary care of Gertrude Baniszewski, a middle-aged single mother and her seven children.

The Baniszewski household was overrun with children. There were few rules and ample freedom. Sadly, the environment created a dangerous hierarchy of social Darwinism where the strong preyed on the weak.

What transpired in the following three months was both riveting and chilling. The case shocked the entire nation and would later be described as "The single worst crime perpetuated against an individual in Indiana's history".

More Books by Ryan Green

On 29th February 2000, John Price took out a restraining order against his girlfriend, Katherine Knight. Later that day, he told his co-workers that she had stabbed him and if he were ever to go missing, it was because Knight had killed him.

The next day, Price didn't show up for work.

A co-worker was sent to check on him. They found a bloody handprint by the front door and they immediately contacted the police. The local police force was not prepared for the chilling scene they were about to encounter.

Price's body was found in a chair, legs crossed, with a bottle of lemonade under his arm. He'd been decapitated and skinned. The "skin-suit" was hanging from a meat hook in the living room and his head was found in the kitchen, in a pot of vegetables that was still warm. There were two plates on the dining table, each had the name of one of Price's children on it.

She was attempting to serve his body parts to his children.

More Books by Ryan Green

In 1902, at the age of 11, Carl Panzram broke into a neighbour's home and stole some apples, a pie, and a revolver. As a frequent troublemaker, the court decided to make an example of him and placed him into the care of the Minnesota State Reform School. During his two-year detention, Carl was repeatedly beaten, tortured, humiliated and raped by the school staff.

At 15-years old, Carl enlisted in the army by lying about his age but his career was short-lived. He was dishonourably discharged for stealing army supplies and was sent to military prison. The brutal prison system sculpted Carl into the man that he would remain for the rest of his life. He hated the whole of mankind and wanted revenge.

When Carl left prison in 1910, he set out to rob, burn, rape and kill as many people as he could, for as long as he could. His campaign of terror could finally begin and nothing could stand in his way.

More Books by Ryan Green

In 1861, the police of a rural French village tore their way into the woodside home of Martin Dumollard. Inside, they found chaos. Paths had been carved through mounds of bloodstained clothing, reaching as high as the ceiling in some places.

The officers assumed that the mysterious maid-robber had killed one woman but failed in his other attempts. Yet, it was becoming sickeningly clear that there was a vast gulf between the crimes they were aware of and the ones that had truly been committed.

Would Dumollard's wife expose his dark secret or was she inextricably linked to the atrocities? Whatever the circumstances, everyone was desperate to discover whether the bloody garments belonged to some of the 648 missing women.

Stay in the loop with the latest releases and exclusive offers by following Ryan!

Follow me:

Facebook	geni.us/ryangreenFB
Instagram	geni.us/ryangreenIG
Amazon	geni.us/ryangreenAM

www.ryangreenbooks.com

Free True Crime Audiobook

Sign up to Audible and use your free credit to download this collection of twelve books. If you cancel within 30 days, there's no charge!

WWW.RYANGREENBOOKS.COM/FREE-AUDIOBOOK

"Ryan Green has produced another excellent book and belongs at the top with true crime writers such as M. William Phelps, Gregg Olsen and Ann Rule" **–B.S. Reid**

"Wow! Chilling, shocking and totally riveting! I'm not going to sleep well after listening to this but the narration was fantastic. Crazy story but highly recommend for any true crime lover!" **–Mandy**

"Torture Mom by Ryan Green left me pretty speechless. The fact that it's a true story is just...wow" **–JStep**

"Graphic, upsetting, but superbly read and written" **–Ray C**

WWW.RYANGREENBOOKS.COM/FREE-AUDIOBOOK